DESSERTED

Recipes *and* Tales *from an* Island Chocolatier

KATE SHAFFER

Photography by
STACEY CRAMP

Design by Miroslaw Jurek
Photographs by Stacey Cramp

Library of Congress
Cataloging-in-Publication Data
Shaffer, Kate.
Desserted : recipes and tales from an island
chocolatier / by Kate Shaffer ;
photography by Stacey Cramp.
p. cm.
Includes index.
ISBN 978-0-89272-991-3
1. Cooking (Chocolate) 2. Cooking--Maine--
Isle au Haut. I. Title.
TX767.C5S48 2011
641.8'6--dc23

2011020868

Printed in China

5   4   3

Down East

Books • Magazine • Online
www.downeast.com
Distributed to the trade
by National Book Network

This book is dedicated to my husband and business partner, Steve, who — according to my refractometer — runs at a steady, cool-headed 88.8 degrees; the perfect tempering agent for a life charted toward unknowable horizons.

Contents

Foreword

Not long ago, I was reluctantly making small talk with a woman whom I was standing behind in an airport security line in Seattle, Washington. When asked, I told her that I am from Maine. She dug deeper, inquiring as to where in Maine I lived. My stock reply, "You've never heard of it," did not suffice, and she insisted upon knowing more. "A small island off the coast," I answered, diverting my eyes as to discourage any further dialogue.

"Which one?" She was relentless.

Well, here goes, I thought. She will either scowl, shrug and agree that the place name is totally foreign to her, or she will recognize both the name and me. The latter scenario usually leads to far more discussion of *The Perfect Storm*, my books, and a certain Discovery Channel television series than I have patience for. "I live on Isle au Haut," I said and crossed my fingers.

The woman's eyes lit up with the excitement of the recognition that I dreaded. "Black Dinah chocolate!" She exclaimed. Stunned and delighted, I nearly initiated a high-five. I now had no reservations, and enthusiastically held up my end of the conversation. I proudly explained that Kate Shaffer is my neighbor and dear friend. We talked island life and chocolate all the way through the security checkpoint and to where we parted ways to find our respective gates. The woman's parting words were, "You are *so* lucky."

When Kate first arrived on Isle au Haut, all I knew about her I learned through the rumor mill. And the grand sum of that was that she had moved to Maine from California. On our island, she may as well have come from Mars. Yet Kate's observations and insights of the island and its people ring as true as the lobsters and blueberries that define our home. Kate writes beautifully of our quirky place with her unique way of articulating a sense of place shared by all islanders. This coupled with some of her chocolate recipes; what a treat!

And to think that up until the time when Kate made her first chocolate, Black Dinah was merely a lump, in fact a poor excuse for a mountain, among a few others that cast rather short shadows on Isle au Haut, or High Island. In the wake of Kate's well-deserved success, Black Dinah denotes something monumental indeed. Black Dinah is the answer to what happens when dreams are pursued. Black Dinah is what results when hard work, perseverance, passion, and raw talent come together. Black Dinah chocolates are the perfect reflection of their creator. They are beautiful. They are simply the best. And the woman in the airport was right. I am *so* lucky.

— *Linda Greenlaw*

Introduction

MAKING A LIVING INTO A LIFE

I first came to the island as a cook. I knew no one, had never had an interest in Isle au Haut beyond a cool job, working for nice folks. Cooking was my only way of moving through this new world, 3,000 miles away from my lifetime home of California. It was that single-mindedness that propelled me through learning the ropes at my new job—a job, the likes of which I had never experienced before. And will never again.

"Are you a school-trained chef?" my new employers, the owners, of the Keepers House Inn, asked me when we first met at their off-island home in the drear of an early Maine spring in 2001.

"No," I answered matter-of-factly, bracing for yet another interview in which I assure my potential employers that I can cook, regardless of my lack of any sort of piece of paper that says I can.

"Good," Jeff Burke breathed. "Those culinary school graduates never last on Isle au Haut."

Jeff and Judi peppered me with questions about my life and what had brought me to Maine. They asked me about my family, about Steve, if I had ever lived on an island before. Did I have children? A dog? Could I chop wood? Did I have a boat?

What they didn't ask me, beyond that first peculiar question, was anything about my life as a cook. I had said I could cook, and that was enough for them. I left the interview puzzled, and curious about a place that required such a quirky set of skills, was home to these gently aging hippies, and yet chewed up and spat out classically trained chefs.

My "try-out" came a month later. It was April, as the winter snows had finally begun to recede on the coast of Maine. I drove through an icy gray fog, in the half-light of a quiet dawn. My dog, an immense Akita/Lab mix, rode shotgun with her nose out the window in the morning air. I found my way unguided through the tiny fishing village of Stonington, to the deserted wood-plank dock, and onto the morning mailboat headed to Isle au Haut. Construction workers stood smoking in the open aft of the boat, sipping from Styrofoam cups of coffee, congregating in affable early morning silence. They greeted me with nods, and grunted a few "ayuh"s when I asked if this was the ferry to Isle au Haut, after which they returned their attention to their cigarettes and coffee and I to the overheated cabin, where I settled in for the sunrise ride out to the tiny island that would, in just a few short years, change the whole course of my life.

My try-out was to make lunch for a work crew of ten men and women who were scattered around the inn property painting, cleaning, cutting up the winter's blow-down,

repairing bicycles, and any number of other tasks required to get the property ready for the new season's guests. Judi led me to the kitchen, showed me where the pots and pans were, how to work the temperamental stove, and left me with a simple, good-natured warning: "Of course, we want it to be delicious, but it's more important that there's a lot. Those people are hungry."

It took me half the morning to take inventory of the unfamiliar kitchen and its ingredients—heavy in dried beans and grains, raw sugars and syrups, organic meats and oils, and a basket full of some early spring gleanings of produce from the mainland grocery.

After a quick refresher course from Judi in the making of fresh bread (after discovering there would be none unless I made it), I got to work on an enormous pot of black bean stew, spiked with smoked chiles and Portuguese sausage; thick, hot slabs of fresh cornbread, fragrant with orange zest and clover honey; a soft oat bread, dark with molasses; and a simple green salad, dressed just as simply with generous drizzles of extra virgin olive oil, red wine vinegar, sea salt, and a few turns of freshly ground pepper.

Lunch was more than an hour late, but the food was hot and hearty, and, most importantly, there was enough of it. I had won myself a job.

I spent the next five years working in that homey kitchen, creating meals that were—if a bit more refined than that first (though not always as successful)—on some level, just as satisfying for both cook and consumer.

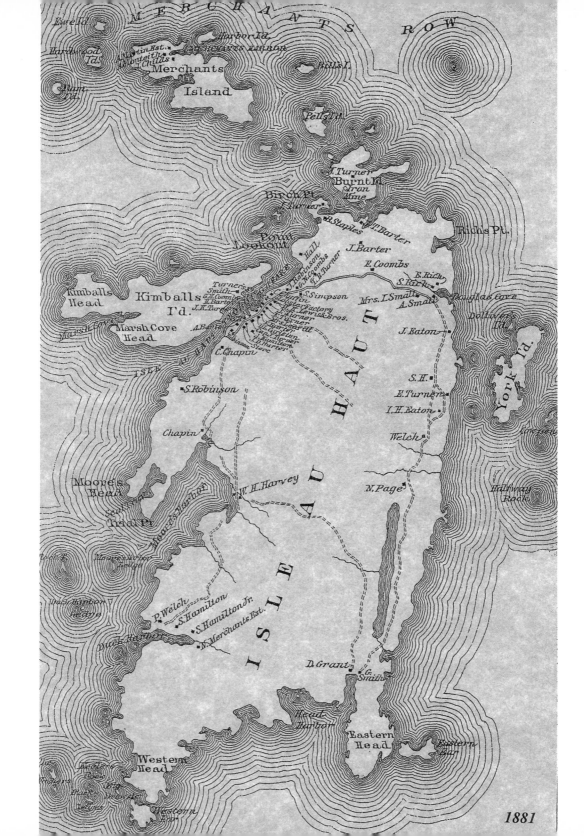

MERCHANTS ROW

Eagle Id.
Hardwood Id.
Martin Est.
McDonald
Childs
Harbor Id.
Merchants Harbor
Merchants Island
Sam Id.
Bills I.
Pell's I'd.

J. Turner
Burnt Id.
Iron Mine
Birch Pt.
T. Turner
Bonny Lookout
B. Staples
T. Barter
Rich's Pt.
J. Barter
E. Coombs
Kimballs Head
Kimballs I'd.
Hall
T. Robinson
W. Coombs
T. B. Turner
S. Simpson
E. Rich
Turner's
Smith
G.W. Coombs
H. Barter
J. K. Turner
A. Barter
S. Kirk
Mrs. I. Small
A. Small
Douglas Cove
Dolliver's I'd.
Marsh Id.
Marsh Cove Head
ISLE AU HAUT
J. Eaton
Post Office
Factory
Lewis & Bros.
Church
Turner
General
Robinson
Hamilton
C. Chapin
Store
E. Harter
York I'd.
C.
S. H.
E. Turner
I. H. Eaton
S. Robinson
Welch
Cow pen
Chapin
Moore's Head
Seal Pt.
Trial Pt.
W. H. Harvey
N. Page
Halfway Rock
Moore's Harbor
Moore's Harbor Ledge
Duck Harbor
Duck Harbor Cove
P. Welch
S. Hamilton
S. Hamilton Jr.
N. Merchants Est.
ISLE AU HAUT
D. Grant
G. Smith
Head Harbor
Eastern Head
Eastern Ear
Western Head
Western

1881

It was also in that kitchen that I developed my baking skills by making bread, pies, and cakes every day from scratch. And it was in that kitchen that I had my first disastrous close encounters with that most aggravating of ingredients: chocolate.

There are no second chances in an island kitchen. If you forget something at the mainland grocery, guess what? You do without. If the farmer doesn't have that case of produce picked in time for you to make the morning mailboat, guess what? You spend the boat ride over figuring out how to sell some very high-paying inn guests on cuisine *sans* vegetables. If the Monday night's fish doesn't make the last boat from Stonington, you have island lobster for the second night in a row. And most importantly, you know the inventory of every cupboard, refrigerator, freezer, and fish crate on the island.

That being said, island kitchens are also the most friendly places on earth. There is always a pot of hot coffee, a stool to sit on, an open cookbook to peruse. There is often a task to help with, and something to learn from a kind cook who is unfettered by the pressure of a restaurant pace or the quest for perfection. Instead, island cooks are governed by the ebb and flow of sunshine, of rain, of gentle gossip, and small-town political intrigue. They plan their menus around a neighbor's birthday, a particularly good catch, a lobsterman's new boat or in anticipation of a contentious town meeting. They are not subject to a particular style or tradition; but rather, they let their menus reflect the peculiar micro culture around them. Island cooks always have an answer to the oft-asked question from a passing tourist: "What is it like to live here?"

Here. Taste. Today, it's like this.

In early 2005, Jeff and Judi announced that they would be retiring and closing the inn at the end of the coming season. I received this news via a crackly telephone conversation in the kitchen of our rented cabin on Isle au Haut. At the time, Steve and I had been navigating our first island nor'easter; a whipping blizzard that left us trapped in our home with frozen pipes, and which had us melting snow for drinking water and morning coffee. The news and the situation were further aggravated by the fact that my aging dog was quickly fading to the pain of bone cancer, and we were facing the surety of her death in the coming days.

Weeks later, in the darkest days of that winter, I found myself restless and alone in my kitchen. Steve had been spending the weekdays working on the mainland while I stayed on the island to write and take reservations via phone and email for the inn's last season. I often turn to my kitchen cupboards for comfort; somehow, the time and focus it takes to make a meal from scratch eases my mind. But at the time, I had no appetite for hearty dinners. Instead, I craved a small bite of something; a morsel with a perfect balance of crunch and softness, of sweet and buttery. And of something else I couldn't quite put my finger on. I tried cookies and biscuits, ice cream, cake. Too much, too little, too sweet, lacking the ingredient I couldn't quite place.

And then I stumbled upon a recipe for chocolate truffles I had torn from the pages of *Gourmet* years before. I had wanted to try it for the inn guests, but the complicated, untried recipe always got shuffled out of my weekly rotation of well-tested standbys.

That recipe took over my tiny cottage kitchen one long winter night: an alchemy of chocolate and cream, butter and egg yolks transformed into a satiny slab of pudding-like ganache that sat atop a pleasingly chewy chocolate brownie base. After allowing the slab to set in the refrigerator, I carefully cut the entire thing into one-inch cubes, and *voila!* Like magic, I had a neat little pile of my very first chocolates.

It's hard to explain how these little truffles became the answer to my unidentified craving. I spent hours just looking at them before I tried one. They were perfectly shaped, consistently sized, and utterly appealing to the eye. At first glance, they all looked exactly alike, but on closer inspection each seemed to express its own tiny personality. I twisted each one into a small square of parchment, then wrapped them in colored tissue paper and tied them with twine. And it wasn't until I had them all packaged for delivery that it occurred to me to try one of the remainders.

That it was delicious wasn't a surprise. That it was what I had been wanting all those weeks, was. I ate one, and I felt better. A lot better.

And so I guess in many ways that's when the seed was planted. That very visceral and emotional reaction to an ingredient I had never thought much about. In the season that followed that winter, chocolate found its way into many dishes at the inn—both sweet and savory. And then it found its way onto my list of possible futures on the island. And then it was the only thing on the list. And then my life began to take shape around it.

The recipes, vignettes, and instructions waiting for you in the following pages tell the story of how it all happened.

— *Kate Shaffer*

Chocolate 101

CHOOSING YOUR CHOCOLATE

When Steve and I got the notion to go into the chocolate business, we knew pretty much zilch about it. All I knew was that if we were going into the chocolate business, then we needed chocolate. So, while Steve was doing the hard work of creating a business model from twigs and island spruce needles, I hopped the morning mailboat and went shopping.

I had a working knowledge of modern chocolate terminology, so when I found myself on the mainland in front of the chocolate counter at my favorite gourmet food store, I had a pretty good idea of what I was looking for. Not that it mattered. I was a woman on a mission, and my mission was to discover the very best chocolate with which to make my truffles. So, I bought every bar in front of me. Oh, and a cup of coffee. And a bottle of wine. The cashier didn't bother with discretion. "Bad day?" she asked.

Since Steve and I weren't making chocolate solely for ourselves, we felt that it would be important to get some other input besides our own. On a quiet mid-winter night, when there was nothing to do on the island but wonder what our neighbors were up to and who they were up to it with, we instead held an informal chocolate tasting. A group that consisted of a handful of lobstermen and carpenters, a boat builder, the school teacher, tax collector, innkeeper, park ranger, lighthouse keeper, and a selectman reported to our small living room for duty, received a brief explanation on how to approach their task, and then got down to work. It was a fairly structured blind tasting; which basically means that I unwrapped all the bars I had bought earlier in the day, laid them out on a numbered grid scribbled onto a large piece of butcher paper, and then handed each taster a sheet that had a table of attributes I wanted them to pay attention to.

After the dust settled, there was a clear winner. And I really, really wish I could tell you that the chocolate that won the taste test that night was the chocolate we ended up ultimately using in our truffles. But it's not. There are, unfortunately, other factors we needed to consider, such as cost and availability, which quickly disqualified several of the chocolates we tried. Instead, second place received the honors, and it ended up being the right choice all around.

So, what does this all mean for you and how you choose the chocolate you use for the recipes in this book—and beyond?

For the most part, all of the chocolate work and recipes described in this book can be done with a quality chocolate you'd probably be able to find on the shelf of your local grocery store. Even our grocery store, which consists of three twelve-foot aisles, is open for two hours, three days a week, and caters to an off-season population of forty-five people, carries chocolates suitable for a batch of French-style truffles.

However, it might help if you make a list of criteria—what you want and don't want in your chocolate—before you start purchasing bars for your tasting. Here are some possible questions to ask yourself:

Is it important that your chocolate be fair trade?

What about organic?

Do you want a single origin chocolate, or is a blend okay?

What's your price range?

How easily can you get it? And how quickly?

These days, buying a bar of chocolate can be as intimidating as buying a bottle of wine. To this, I say, "Whatever." Here's the deal: if it tastes good, it is good. And by that I mean that I've found that Vianne Rocher (the beautiful chocolateur in the luscious movie *Chocolat*) was right: everyone really does have a favorite, and it rarely has anything to do with how much it costs, how shiny the label is, and whether or not it has a French name. Most of us, if we're breathing, have been eating chocolate since we were babies. We learned to like it before we knew how to explain why we liked it, or what exactly we liked about it. I call this the Zen mind of chocolate. We don't have to learn, as with wine, what we like and don't like. We already have a developed palate with chocolate; we already know what we like.

WHAT EXACTLY IS CHOCOLATE?

Chocolate comes from the seeds of a cacao tree, *Theobroma cacao*, native to tropical regions of the Americas and cultivatable in regions between zero and twenty degrees latitude, north or south of the equator.

Modern chocolate making is basically a six-step process, which is still, surprisingly, much like how it all began.

STEP 1: HARVEST AND SEED EXTRACTION

The fruit of the cacao tree are ridged football-shaped pods that vary in color from green to yellow/orange and red. They grow directly out of the trunk of the tree and are harvested by hand by knocking them off the trunk with a stick or by cutting them off with a machete. The pods are then split lengthwise (again, usually with a machete) to expose a mass of almond-size seeds encased in a sticky white mucilage.

STEP 2: FERMENTATION

Next, the seeds (or beans, as they are more commonly called) are scooped out of the pod and heaped in a pile or into wooden crates to ferment. The heat created by fermentation helps to melt off the gooey white stuff, so that all is left is the seed. The heat also kills the germination process and is key to beginning to develop the full flavor of the seed. This process takes anywhere between three and nine days.

Step 3: Drying

After fermenting, the beans are spread onto racks—either freestanding racks or roof-mounted ones—or tossed out onto roads or whatever flat surface is available in great quantities, and allowed to dry in the sun. Drying takes from seven to thirty days.

Step 4: Roasting

After drying, the beans are ready to roast. Some producers choose to age their beans for a quantity of time before roasting. The benefit of aging is primarily flavor development, and those who employ this practice feel that it is key to the quality of their final product. But whether or not the producer chooses to age their beans or not, roasting is where the true art of chocolate production takes flight.

Step 5: Sorting, Flinging, and Conching

Once the beans are roasted to the producer's specifications, the beans are sorted and then placed in a bean flinger (yes, that's the technical term). The flinger cracks off the hull of the bean, so all that is left is the nib—essentially, the meat of the bean. The nibs are then placed in a conche—sort of like a burr coffee grinder multiplied by a million—which grinds the beans down into a fluid mass that is kept liquefied by frictional heat. This fluid mass is called chocolate liquor, and while that made me pretty excited, too, the first time I heard the term, it has nothing to do with alcohol. Conching reduces the cocoa mass into particles too small to be detected by the human tongue. How small these particles get are a factor in the quality of the final product. The smaller the particles, the smoother the mouthfeel of the chocolate.

Step 6: Tempering and Molding

Depending on what kind of chocolate the producer is making (dark, milk, or unsweetened), sugar, vanilla, milk powder (if making milk chocolate), and, in most cases, soy lecithin (used as an emulsifying agent, which also helps with mouthfeel), are added to the chocolate liquor. The melted mass is then heated and cooled very carefully—a process called tempering—and poured into molds to form bricks or bars (or whatever shape the producers sells its final product in), cooled until set, and then released from the molds and packaged.

Chocolate Terminology

Cocoa butter: This is the highly valued fat from the cocoa bean. Cocoa butter is produced by pressing the beans to separate the fat from the solids. The by-product of this process is cocoa powder.

Natural cocoa powder: This is the result of extracting the fat from the cocoa bean, and then grinding what's left into a powder.

Dutched or Dutch-process cocoa powder: This is cocoa powder treated with an alkaline substance in order to reduce acidity and darken the color. Dutch-process cocoa powder is more readily dissolved in liquids such as water or milk.

Unsweetened chocolate: Remember the chocolate liquor created in Step Five above? Well, this is it. Unadulterated chocolate that may or may not have extra cocoa butter or soy lecithin added to it. But never sugar or milk. The form you buy at the market has been tempered and molded into bars, and is often called baking chocolate or cooking chocolate.

Dark chocolate: This is cocoa liquor, some amount of sugar, usually vanilla, and sometimes soy lecithin. Basically, there are two types of dark chocolate: bittersweet and semisweet. For the most part, the two can be used interchangeably.

Bittersweet chocolate: This is a slightly sweetened dark chocolate that, according to the FDA, contains no less than 35% cocoa.

Semisweet chocolate: This is dark chocolate that has more sugar than bittersweet chocolate.

Milk chocolate: This is chocolate that contains, according to the FDA, no less than 10% cocoa solids and 12% milk solids.

White chocolate: This is chocolate that contains cocoa butter, milk solids, and sugar, but no cocoa solids.

Cacao: Technically, this is what cocoa beans are called before they are roasted. However, the term is now used interchangeably with cocoa.

COUVERTURE: Dark chocolate to which the producer has added extra cocoa butter is called couverture. Confectioners (like me) use it for the coating chocolate on French-style truffles and it is the chocolate we use to line and seal our molds for Belgian-style truffles. Because of its extra-high fat content, couverture is usually not suitable for baking. Not that I haven't tried. And this, above all else, is why I know.

SINGLE-ORIGIN CHOCOLATE: This is chocolate made from beans that have been grown in a single region of the world. For instance, if a label specifies Venezuela or Columbia, then that means the beans used to produce that chocolate have been grown in those regions. It does not necessarily mean that the chocolate has been produced there.

ESTATE CHOCOLATE: This is chocolate made from beans grown on a single farm or estate.

It sometimes also helps to know what is *not* chocolate. Summer coat, compound chocolate, "candy melts," and any "chocolate" made with anything other than the ingredients listed above, is not chocolate. A substance made with, say, partially hydrogenated vegetable fat instead of cocoa butter, does not follow the same rules as chocolate, will not behave the same way, and is an inferior product. Fake chocolate is just that: fake. And while I like an Elvis impersonator as much as the next gal, in the world of chocolate, there just ain't nothin' like the real thing.

A CHOCOLATE CONSCIENCE

Chocolate can be grown only in very few regions of the planet—those lands that lie between zero and twenty degrees north or south of the equator. Look at a map. See where this is? Many of these regions are in places that have recently been or are currently plagued with civil unrest, dicey human rights policies, war, slavery, and an alarmingly poor environmental conservation record. Unfortunately, cacao growers often take advantage of these situations and use slack labor laws and questionable agricultural practices to cheaply produce a commodity that they can, in turn, sell for large profits. I implore you to research not only the company that produces the chocolate that you use, but also where the beans themselves come from. There are some great companies out there that are using cacao and its universal appeal to do good in areas of the world that desperately need it.

Chocolate makes us smile. So it makes sense that it should bring joy to the human and animal communities in which it is grown and produced.

CREATING (AND KEEPING) GOOD TEMPER WITH CHOCOLATE
(OR, WHAT CHOCOLATE MAKING AND TOWN MEETING HAVE IN COMMON)

There are several recipes in this book that call for melted and "tempered" chocolate. Tempered chocolate is not a special kind of chocolate that you need to order from a fancy gourmet food company. It is simply chocolate that you have done something special to—a very particular process of melting and cooling so that it sets and hardens smoothly, with a fine sheen and no blemishes. Tempering is not particularly difficult to do, but it is very hard to get right. And yet, it is an absolutely necessary skill to have if you want to create chocolates that are as good to look at as they are to eat.

Around Christmastime, food magazines often feature candy recipes that call for chocolate that has been melted and tempered. When I started teaching chocolate-making classes, I paid very close attention to how these magazines explained the process of tempering. Many of these instructions I found to be incorrect or misleading; some were overly simplified; and other magazines left out tempering instructions altogether, leaving the reader to fend for him- or herself. Admittedly, it is very hard to tell someone how to temper chocolate without showing them as well. But still, I figured there had to be a better way.

In 2008, I had the wonderful opportunity to attend a week-long professional chocolate-making workshop given by a gifted instructor from Ecole Chocolat in Vancouver, British Columbia. Our instructor accompanied her demonstration on tempering with a very clever real-life analogy, and it got me thinking about how the tempering process was so similar to many real-life situations, both literally and metaphorically. Even right here on Isle au Haut. So I will begin this tutorial with a story.

The *Annual Town Report*, the islander's harbinger of spring, appears in the island store right around the first week in March every year. Who needs daffodils and fuzzy baby bunnies to tell us that winter's over when we've got 104 typewritten pages of scintillating town factoids? This little gem is packed full of goodies: Like what the town spent money on, how the annual summer library bake sale went, who hasn't paid their property taxes, and what the proposed budget for the upcoming fiscal year is. It's a much anticipated study guide for islanders as they get ready for town meeting, always scheduled for the last Monday in March.

There is no event more ill-timed, in my opinion, than the Isle au Haut town meeting. After four months of being stranded on an inclement rock in the middle of the ocean with just forty-two other adults—some of whom you wouldn't necessarily share dinner, much less an opinion—it's just a bad idea to throw us all in a room together and demand that we decide the future of our town. No, we don't all get along. And by the end of March, we're all going a little nuts, and, quite frankly, there are a few people I've met over the years who I wouldn't mind throwing overboard to test their buoyancy, if you know what I mean.

Town meeting is an all-day event beginning promptly at 8:30 A.M. Work is put aside and townspeople are asked to contribute food to snack on throughout the day. Lisa Turner brings her 100-cup percolater (and, if we're really lucky, she also brings her fish chowder), and everything is piled up on a table just below the town hall stage.

Some years the meeting warrant has more than one-hundred articles, and because our community is so small, and tempers can run hot, all articles concerning the election of town officials (roughly twenty-five) are cast by written ballot. That's right: we write it down on a little piece of paper, walk up to the front of the hall, and place the paper in a wooden box. This in an effort to keep our voting anonymous. But it's all for appearances; the votes for contentious elections have been counted up on notepads around dinner tables the night before.

Some years ago, town meeting fell on the day after Easter. The night before, we had dined on baked ham and a vegetarian pasticcio with several other folks at the home of Al Gordon and Kathie Fiveash. Kathie made a homey lemon sponge pudding for dessert, and we ate it with heaping spoonfuls of softly whipped cream. We shared the leftovers with the rest of the community the next day.

Whenever I start to dread the end of March, I remember that Easter meal at Al and Kathie's, what it feels like to share a meal with good friends, and then to break bread again the next day with folks with whom, though we may not always see eye to eye, we share a common goal of consensus, sustainability, and cohesion.

Which, amazingly, has everything in the world to do with chocolate. Let me explain.

Pick up your favorite bar of chocolate from your local grocery store. When you get home, unwrap the bar and take a good look at it. It should be glossy and unmarred. No cracks or gray haze, streaks or spots. The color of it should be uniform.

Now break off a chunk. That shouldn't be easy, but the break should be clean and the chocolate should make a sharp snapping noise. It shouldn't crumble or fall apart.

This bar—and any bar you buy off the shelf—is in temper. Technically this means that all the fat crystals in the bar are stable and in perfect alignment. It is a state that every confectioner strives for when working with chocolate, to be able to create a finished product that looks beautiful and possesses strength and integrity of substance.

Now, pretend that this bar of chocolate is a community of people. This bar is an example of the community in an ideal state. We are maintaining a common consensus, working towards a common goal (keeping the island together), and damn it, we look good together. We are in good temper.

Every year at town meeting, we try and create new goals for our town. In the weeks leading up to the meeting, we introduce certain elements to our community that start breaking our temper. Like the *town report*. Or rumors about who is going to try and unseat whom for the position of selectman. Or treasurer. Or school committee member. There are secret meetings and whispered accusations. Community members split off and form splinter groups, things heat up, and the community begins to break apart.

As confectioners, if we want to create something new from our bar of chocolate, but keep the same desirable qualities (gloss, structural integrity), we must begin by breaking the bar apart and melting it down; thus destroying its temper.

It may seem counterproductive to destroy the very qualities we want to maintain, but the process is absolutely necessary if we want to forge something new out of the bar. Fortunately, there is a way to reclaim those qualities. The trick is, when we break up the bar, we set a little pile of pieces aside, and then melt down the rest. Those reserved pieces will be our "seed," and we will introduce them to our heated up, melted chocolate in order to cool down the whole mass and bring it back into temper.

By the time the residents of Isle au Haut arrive at the town hall on the last Monday in March, we have worked ourselves up into a good hot lather, and the hall itself is our melting pot. We enter, and there are several moments of emotional chaos as opposing candidates and their supporters come face to face, as we try and quell our passions regarding a particular warrant item while we politely greet our neighbors, as we inadvertently scan the room for a particular hot head, or for a voter who is famous for keeping their cool. And then the meeting is called to order, we take our seats, and we perform our first act of bringing our community back into temper; we vote in a moderator.

For those of you who are familiar with the New England town meeting, you know that it is essential that the moderator be calm, cool, and collected at all times, and yet authoritative enough to be able to create and maintain order in a heated, sometimes hostile environment. Our candidate is always Reverend Ted Hoskins. We vote him in, he steps up to the podium, takes the gavel, and with his calm voice and powerful presence, he begins the long process of helping our community navigate a warrant of potentially contentious articles and reach consensus. Slowly, throughout the day, Ted eases conflict, facilitates discussions, and helps to bring dissenting parties into contact and constructive debate with one another. And each time he succeeds with one person, that person can do the same with another. This chain reaction ultimately leads us to completing the voting on the entire warrant, and our town is ready to forge ourselves into the shape we choose.

Ted Hoskins is our "seed" chocolate—the little pile of broken pieces from the bar that we set aside for later. These pieces are still in temper, so when we introduce them to the melted mass of chocolate, they will have a stabilizing affect on it. And they do this in much the same way that Ted does at town meeting. They cool the mass down, come into contact with other fat crystals, and help stabilize the less cooperative ones; which, in turn, go off to stabilize more uncooperative fat crystals. Eventually, with enough stirring and enough time to allow the mass to cool, all the fat crystals will come into alignment with each other, and our chocolate will be in temper.

HOW TO TEMPER CHOCOLATE

Now that you know the basic philosophy behind tempering, here are some step-by-step instructions. Don't expect to get it right the first time. Or the second. And don't expect to get it right every time. But the more you do it, the more you will understand it. And the more you understand it, the more consistently successful your results will be.

You'll need: kitchen thermometer, saucepan, metal bowl (the metal bowl needs to be able to fit on top of the saucepan), rubber spatula, and 12 ounces or more of a quality chocolate with a high percentage of cocoa butter.

Tempering Tip: Make sure your ingredients, tools, and work environment are completely dry during the entire process. Even a small amount of water will turn your smooth liquid chocolate into a sticky, lumpy mess. Also, be sure that your kitchen is not too hot. Seventy degrees is an ideal temperature for working with chocolate.

STEP 1: Fill the saucepan ⅓ of the way with water and heat to almost a boil. You want the water to be steaming hot, but don't let it boil. Remove the pan from the heat.

STEP 2: Get out your chocolate. If it is not already cut up, cut it into small pieces of equal size.

STEP 3: Set aside ⅓ of the chocolate (this will be your seed chocolate). Put the remaining ⅔ of the chocolate into your metal bowl and place the bowl on top of the saucepan. You may use a double boiler for this, but it's important to make sure that the water never directly touches the bottom of the bowl. The chocolate should slowly begin to melt. Try not to disturb the chocolate during this process. A few stirs with a rubber spatula near the end of the process should help mix the melted chocolate.

STEP 4: As the chocolate melts, monitor the temperature with your thermometer. The melting temperature of the chocolate will vary depending on the manufacturer, but should not exceed 125 degrees for bittersweet chocolate, or 115 degrees for milk or white chocolate. As soon as the chocolate has melted, remove the bowl from the saucepan. Use a towel to wipe away moisture from the bottom of the bowl. This will prevent any water from finding its way into the bowl. Water will seize the chocolate and can ruin the batch.

STEP 5: Place the bowl on a table and add ⅓ of your seed chocolate to the bowl. Stir until the introduced chocolate completely melts. Take another third and repeat the process. Monitor the temperature of the chocolate as you mix it. You should notice the temperature drop as you add each batch of seed to the mass.

STEP 6: Add the last batch of seed, and as the temperature drops, start conducting temper checks every few minutes by dribbling a bit of chocolate onto your metal icing spatula. Using the rubber spatula, mix the chocolate until all of it is completely melted. If it is in temper, the chocolate will quickly harden on your icing spatula to an even, satiny sheen, with no streaks or spots. The resulting temperature of your chocolate should be between 85 and 90 degrees.

WORKING WITH (AND MAINTAINING) TEMPER

Now that our chocolate is in temper and yet still fluid, we have the ability to do all sorts of things with it—dip pieces of ganache to make truffles; dip cookies, pretzels, nuts; pour into molds to make beautiful glossy shapes; pipe into designs on parchment to make decorations that we can use later. The possibilities are only limited by your imagination. That, and your ability to keep the chocolate in temper and yet still fluid enough to work with, for as long as it takes to complete your task. This can prove to be a bit tricky since stable fat crystals have the tendency to grow more stable fat crystals. Eventually there will be so many stable crystals in our mass of chocolate that it will be too thick to work with. There's an easy fix, though, so don't worry.

All we need is a good blast of heat to break the temper of some of the mass. There are many ways you can do this, but by far, the easiest and quickest way I have found, is to shoot a direct blast of heat onto the surface of the chocolate with a hair dryer. Hold the hair dryer as close to the surface of the chocolate as possible and, depending on the amount of chocolate you're working with, apply heat for anywhere between a few seconds to several minutes. Next, stir the mass of chocolate thoroughly so that the area that you've just knocked out of temper comes into contact with remaining mass of stable crystals. Do a temper check to make sure you're back in temper, and then continue your task. After this quick blast of heat, the chocolate should be fluid enough for you to continue working.

BASIC COATING TECHNIQUES

COATING TECHNIQUE FOR ROUND TRUFFLES: To ensure complete coverage, round truffles should first be coated in a thin layer of chocolate before dipping. Place a small amount of chocolate in the palm of one hand, and then with the other hand, roll a truffle—palms facing each other—until the entire ball is coated in a very thin layer of chocolate. Roll the coated ball onto a parchment-lined tray, and allow to set before dipping. Every few truffles or so, scrape any excess chocolate from your hands (I do this by scraping my palms on the lip of my bowl) and repeat the process.

Alternatively, after coating the truffle, roll it onto a pie tin filled with a shallow layer of cocoa powder, granulated sugar, shredded coconut, finely ground nuts, or whatever else you can think of. Keeping the pie tin flat on the counter, shimmy the tin in a circular motion so that the truffle rolls around and becomes completely coated. Remove to a parchment-lined tray and allow to set.

DIPPING TECHNIQUE FOR ROUND TRUFFLES: Place your coated truffle on the surface of the tempered chocolate. With your index and middle fingers held together, push down on the ball and submerge it completely, then scoop it out of the bowl using an arcing motion, so that your truffle ends up balanced on top of your fingers. Next, gently slap the back sides of your fingers on the surface of the chocolate two or three times (this motion will pull any excess chocolate from your fingers). Then, transfer the truffle to a parchment-lined tray by carefully—but quickly—flipping it over so that the top of the truffle becomes the bottom. Gently pull your fingers from the top of the truffle, and move them in a small circular motion to create a tiny flourish on top of the truffle. While the chocolate is still wet, you may sprinkle with any variety of garnishes—sprinkles, nuts, coconut, etc. — and then allow the truffles to set at room temperature.

DIPPING TECHNIQUE FOR RECTANGULAR OR SQUARE TRUFFLES ("PALETTES"): Because you will have "bottomed" your palettes with a layer of tempered chocolate, there is no need to coat them with chocolate before dipping (as with round truffles).

Place the palette, bottomed side down, onto the surface of your tempered chocolate. With a dinner fork (or a truffle-dipping fork, if you have one), scoop tempered chocolate over the entire palette. Then place your fork under the palette and gently lift it out of the chocolate. Remove excess chocolate by gently slapping the bottom of your fork onto the surface of the chocolate. Transfer the truffle onto a parchment-lined tray by tilting the fork away from you and allowing the truffle to slide off. Once the edge of the truffle comes into contact with the parchment, gently pull away your fork, allowing the truffle to settle gently onto the tray. While the chocolate is still wet, you may top your truffles with your choice of garnish.

SETTING THE CHOCOLATE

Once we've dipped a truffle or a cookie with our hard-won tempered chocolate, it would be a shame to then leave it unattended only to have it fall out of temper as it hardens. This would result in a confection that is gray, streaked or dull; cakey or crumbly, and generally unappetizing to the eye. Oh, it would still taste delicious, but we didn't go through all that hard work to make it taste good—it already tasted good. We went through all that work so that our finished piece of chocolate looks beautiful.

Chocolate depends on an exothermic reaction to crystallize properly. That means it has to get rid of its heat quickly and evenly. Unfortunately, chocolate has a hard time cooling off. This is further aggravated by less than desirable environmental conditions, like a hot room or a humid day. If all you've done is use the chocolate to coat truffles or cookies, and your room is about 70 degrees or cooler, your pieces will be fine setting at room temperature. However, if you have made molded pieces or nut clusters, you will need to help the chocolate by allowing it to set in your refrigerator for anywhere between 5 and 25 minutes. Once the chocolate hardens, it will be fine completing crystallization at room temperature. Complete crystallization takes about 24 hours, though you may handle (or eat) your chocolates before them.

Problem Solving

Some of the recipes in this book are easy, but I'm not going to lie to you: working with chocolate isn't exactly a walk in the park. Some recipes, such as those in the Truffles chapter, require a very specialized set of skills; skills that most professional chefs don't even possess—not because they're particularly difficult, but because they are completely useless for any application other than chocolate.

I urge you to try and remember that the very best way in the world to learn anything is by screwing it up over and over and over again. This, above all else, is how I learned to do what I do. I made mistakes. And then I learned how to fix them. Here are some helpful hints for common mistakes.

....

PROBLEM: I have blitzed my ganache in the food processor, and now it looks like a pile of mud with an enormous oil slick on top.

EXPLANATION: Your ganache has "split." That is to say, the fat has separated from the solids, and your emulsion has failed.

POSSIBLE REMEDY: It's very likely that the ganache is either too warm or too cool to emulsify properly. Take its temperature with your kitchen thermometer. It should be right around 90 degrees. If it is warmer than 90, wait for it to cool down, and then give it another go with the food processor. It should come together within a few minutes. If it is too cool, give it a good blast of heat with a hair dryer, then re-process. If neither of these things works, and the temperature of your ganache is correct, try adding a bit of spirit (whiskey, rum, vodka, whatever you've got that won't taste weird with chocolate) to the mixture, and process again.

....

PROBLEM: My ganache crumbles and/or cracks when I try to cut it into squares.

EXPLANATION: It probably wasn't completely emulsified when you spread it in the pan.

POSSIBLE REMEDY: Break up the ganache and slowly melt it down in a metal bowl over a pot of hot water while stirring intermittently. When the ganache has almost completely melted, remove the bowl from the heat and continue stirring. The emulsion should come together (remember, it should have a smooth, pudding-like texture), at which point you can return it to the brownie pan, level it, and allow it to set overnight.

....

PROBLEM: My ganache is gooey and just too soft to work with.

EXPLANATION: It may be that your room is too warm for the ganache to crystallize properly.

REMEDY: Try allowing the ganache to set in the refrigerator, and then have it come to room temperature before dipping. You may need to reconstitute your ganache by melting it down and re-emulsifying it for this to work properly.

PROBLEM: My ganache is still gooey.

EXPLANATION: It's possible that there is not enough cocoa butter in your chocolate.

REMEDY: If you are especially attached to the chocolate you are using, try cutting down on the cream or other liquids in the recipe (purees, etc.).

....

PROBLEM: My finished truffles have a whitish or grayish haze all over them.

EXPLANATION: Your chocolate was not in good temper when you dipped your truffles, or they were allowed to set in a room that was too warm, and were knocked out of temper after you dipped them.

REMEDY: Well, the good news is that your truffles will still be delicious. The "bloom" on the surface of the chocolate does not affect the taste, so pile them up and serve them for dessert. Next, re-visit your tempering process and try, try again. Make sure you do a temper check before you start dipping. It may not give you the results you want, but it will give you the opportunity to correct it before you dip your truffles. Also, make sure the temperature of your room is not above 70 degrees. If it is, you may need to use your refrigerator to set your chocolate. See the chapter on tempering.

....

PROBLEM: My chocolate is still lumpy after melting it.

EXPLANATION: It's likely that you've overheated your chocolate.

REMEDY: It will not be suitable for tempering, however you may use it in a baking application. Remember to melt your chocolate in a bowl that is set over (but not touching) a pan of hot water. It is also best if your pan is not over direct heat while you are in the process of melting your chocolate.

....

PROBLEM: My melted chocolate suddenly turned into a dry, unworkable mess.

EXPLANATION: Your chocolate has "seized." Somehow, a drop of water or a particle of steam has found its way into your chocolate and caused all the trouble.

REMEDY: It will not be suitable for tempering, however, if you add more liquid (water, cream, coffee, whatever) and a little butter, you may create a nice chocolate sauce from your seized chocolate. Stir in the liquid while still over your hot water, and the whole thing will eventually smooth out.

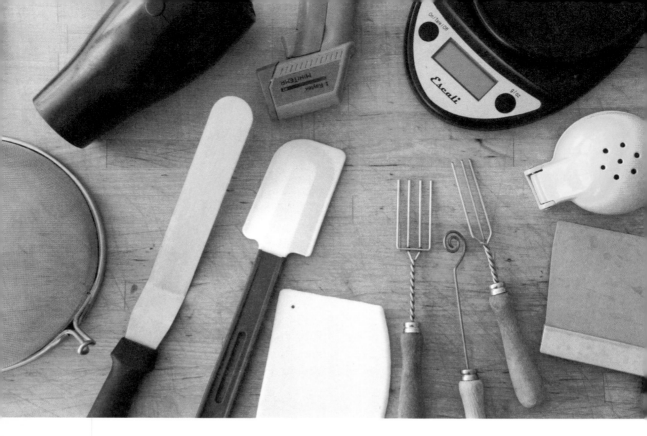

TOOLBOX

Since 2007, Steve and I have been operating our growing company from our home kitchen on Isle au Haut. At the time of this writing (January 2011), we are in the middle of building a new commercial kitchen in a detached barn on our property. However, for four years, we have managed to meet consumer demand, producing roughly 150,000 chocolates per year, with no specialized machinery.

While I don't recommend it, this experience has cemented my belief that anyone can work successfully with chocolate using very common tools in a small home kitchen. That being said, the following is a list of items that will make your work easier and more enjoyable.

DIPPING FORKS: While you can always use a regular dinner fork to dip your truffles, dipping forks have narrower tines that are spread farther apart than normal forks, and so make it easier to slide your truffle off the fork. You can find dipping forks at most gourmet cooking stores.

HAIR DRYER: If you have read the previous chapters, then you already know how essential this tool is. In fact, if I had to pick a tool I could not live without in my kitchen, this would be it. Buy the cheapest one you can find, and use it for everything from loosening up over-tempered chocolate to reconstituting ganache or buttercream.

KITCHEN SCALE: Purchase one with a digital display.

KITCHEN THERMOMETER: Find one that has a digital display and a slender sensor with a long cord.

REFRACTOMETER: While not a requirement by any means, this handy little tool has revolutionized my chocolate work. With a pull of a trigger, a refractometer will take an instant surface temperature of chocolate, ganache, soup, or your spouse. And it eliminates the frustration of stirring around a kitchen thermometer.

BENCH SCRAPERS: The metal ones are essential for mixing scone, bread, piecrust or cinnamon roll dough. The plastic ones are great for scraping out bread bowls.

DRYWALL SPATULA: Serves much the same purpose as a bench scraper, but is less expensive and has a long handle, making it easier to grasp and maneuver.

METAL ICING SPATULAS: Essential for frosting a cake or conducting a temper check.

FOOD PROCESSOR: I have found that I have consistently successful results when I emulsify my ganaches in a food processor. In all of my truffle recipes, my instructions assume that you have this tool. You may, of course, make a successful ganache without one, but a food processor will make the process a wee bit easier.

STAND MIXER: While there is only one recipe in this book that absolutely requires this tool, a stand mixer will change your baking life forever.

JUICER: I use a juicer to make silky fruit purees that give the most bang for the buck in flavor.

SIEVE: An important tool for straining out the ingredients in an infusion, or for making seedless fruit purees (in the absence of a juicer).

A STURDY SET OF METAL BOWLS

SEVERAL HEAT-PROOF RUBBER SPATULAS

VINYL OR LATEX GLOVES: While I think it's important not to desensitize ourselves to militant hygiene while working in the kitchen, I have recently adopted the use of skin-tight latex gloves to protect my hands from the drying effects of constant hand-washing and certain ingredients.

PANTRY BASICS

Throughout this book, there are certain ingredients printed in bold type. These refer to a few homemade pantry basics that I find helpful to have on hand. None of them are particularly hard to make, and all of them can be replaced with a store-bought substitution, but for the best flavor and texture in your confections and baked goods, I recommend building up a small homemade supply of the following ingredients.

INVERT SUGAR: Used widely in confectionery to improve texture and shelf life, invert sugar syrup is the result when sucrose (granulated sugar) is split into its two components, glucose and fructose. Place two parts granulated sugar and one part water into a saucepan and bring to a simmer. Stir briefly to make sure that all the sugar is dissolved. Add 2 teaspoons lemon juice for every pound of granulated sugar in your formula. Simmer gently for 20 minutes without stirring, cool completely, and store in an airtight jar.

CARAMEL SAUCE, PAGE 38

RASPBERRY AND STRAWBERRY PUREE: For best results, buy your fruit in season and process immediately. If you have an electric juicer, put the fruit through until all you have in the mulch pile are seeds. Depending on the quality of your juicer, this may take up to 4 or 5 times. Alternatively, process the fresh fruit in a food processor, and then press the puree through a fine sieve or put through a food mill. For long-term storage, freeze the puree in zippered freezer bags, laying them flat so they take up as little space as possible. To concentrate the puree (as for the Wild Raspberry Truffles recipe), place the puree in a saucepan and simmer until it is reduced by half.

PUMPKIN PUREE: Making your own pumpkin puree is a bit labor intensive, but the work pays off in flavor and texture. Purchase pie pumpkins or creamy-fleshed winter squashes (such as butternut) in season, and if the grower hasn't cured them already, allow them to stand at room temperature for 10 to 20 days. Depending on the shape of the squash, either cut in half lengthwise, or quarter, and scoop out the seeds. Bake, flesh side down, on a parchment-lined half sheet pan at 350 degrees until the fruit is very soft. Remove from the oven (reducing the temperature to 250 degrees) and when the squash is cool enough to handle, scoop the flesh into a food processor and whir until it is completely smooth. Line your sheet pans with new parchment, and spread the puree about ½ inch thick over the entire surface of the pan. Bake the puree, stirring and re-spreading several times (to prevent browning), until the squash is paste-like, but not dry. Give the puree one last blitz in the food processor before packing into freezer bags and freezing.

Caramel Sauce MAKES 4 CUPS

1 ⅓ CUPS SUGAR

1 CUP CORN SYRUP

½ VANILLA BEAN

1 ¾ CUPS HEAVY CREAM

4 TABLESPOONS UNSALTED BUTTER

¼ CUP HONEY

½ TEASPOON SEA SALT

Combine the sugar, corn syrup, and ¼ cup of water in a large, heavy saucepan. Split and scrape the seeds from the vanilla bean and add them to the saucepan. Toss in the split pod as well. Cook the mixture over high heat, stirring occasionally, until it reaches 295 degrees on a candy thermometer.

While the sugars are cooking, place the cream in a medium saucepan and bring to a boil over low heat. Keep the cream warm.

When the sugar mixture reaches 295 degrees, reduce the heat to low and add the butter, honey, hot cream, and sea salt. Use caution and wear and oven mitt as you do this: the mixture will boil and spit with enthusiasm. Stir to fully combine the ingredients, turn the heat up slightly, and cook for 5 more minutes. Remove the pan from the heat, pluck out the vanilla bean pod with tongs, and allow the caramel to cool completely before putting it into a jar and storing in the refrigerator.

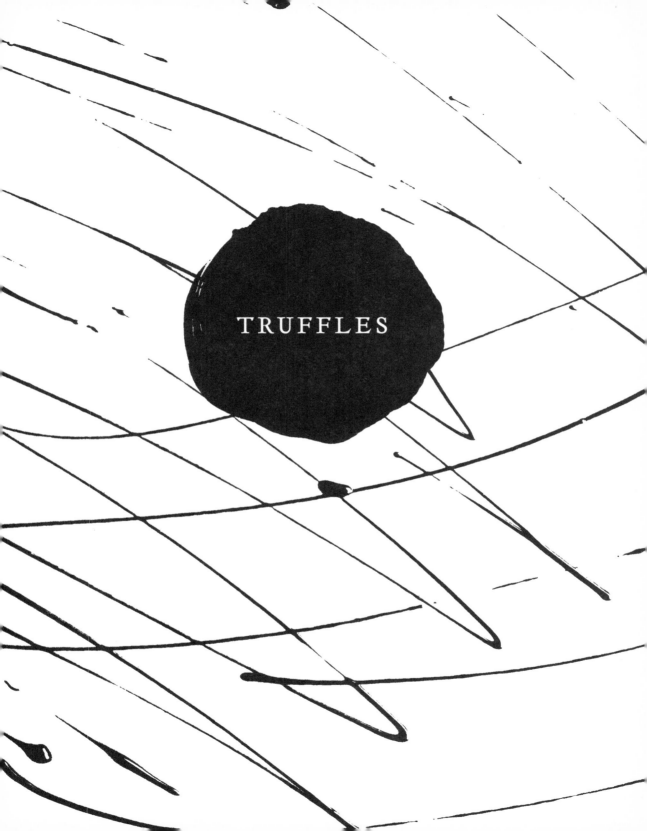

TRUFFLES

Bittersweet Chocolate Truffles

Several years ago, while searching for a chocolate to replace the one I was having increasing difficulty getting from a once-wonderful small company that had recently been absorbed by a multi-national conglomerate, I had the opportunity to sample a single-origin chocolate from Peru. One taste, and I knew I had my replacement. And after months of cursing the evil powers of hegemony and greed that dictate valuable third-world commodities such as chocolate, I found myself, instead, thanking them for the opportunity to discover La Orquidea, a small, worker-owned cooperative in Peru that makes some of the finest chocolate on the planet. If you have a favorite bittersweet chocolate, this is the recipe to showcase it. If possible, use the same chocolate for coating the truffles as you do in the ganache. MAKES 64 TRUFFLES

⋯⋯

2¾ POUNDS BITTERSWEET CHOCOLATE

2 OUNCES INVERT SUGAR (PAGE 36) OR MILD HONEY

¾ CUP HEAVY CREAM

5 TABLESPOONS VERY SOFT UNSALTED BUTTER

⋯⋯

Chop 12 ounces of the chocolate and place it in a food processor. Pour the invert sugar or honey on top of the chocolate.

Place the cream in a small saucepan and bring to a full boil over medium heat.

Once the cream boils, pour it immediately over the chopped chocolate. Allow the cream to sit for a minute or two, then process the mixture for about 30 seconds. Add the butter in small chunks, then whir until the mixture is completely smooth and emulsified and falls off of a rubber spatula in thick blobs. It should be the consistency of pudding. Do not over process, or your ganache will separate.

Scrape the emulsified ganache into a plastic-wrap–lined 8"x8" brownie pan. Level the ganache carefully with an offset icing spatula, spreading it all the way to the sides and completely into the corners. Allow the ganache to set at a cool room temperature (or in the refrigerator if your house is very warm) overnight.

When the ganache is set, and you are ready to finish your truffles, chop the remaining 2 pounds of bittersweet chocolate. Melt and temper the chocolate (see pages 28–30).

Remove the ganache from the pan by lifting it out by the plastic wrap. "Bottom" your ganache by spreading a very thin layer of tempered chocolate on the entire top surface of the ganache. When the chocolate has set, turn the slab over and cut it into 1" squares.

Dip the squares, chocolate side down, into the tempered chocolate using a dipping fork (see page 31).

Alternatively, skip the "bottoming" step and roll the ganache, instead, into walnut size balls and dip or decorate as desired (see page 31).

TRUFFLES, by definition, are a fresh dairy product. In their most basic form, truffles are walnut-size balls of ganache—a mixture of heavy cream and chocolate. When coated with a thin layer of chocolate and dusted with cocoa powder, truffles not only resemble their namesake (the coveted fungus that grows in the ground), but are also shelf-stable at a cool room temperature for a limited time. There is a long scientific explanation as to why this is true, but I can tell you that it has to do with water, and slowing down its movement within the ganache. When we create a stable emulsion of cream and chocolate, in which those ingredients are held in perfect suspension with one another, the water activity in the cream (which is what makes the cream susceptible to bacterial growth) slows way down. We can further slow water activity by the judicious addition of liquid sweeteners, which bind water molecules. To protect our ganache from air—another source of bacteria—we can coat our truffles in chocolate. After we have thus armored our truffles, they will be good at a cool room temperature for up to two weeks.

You may prolong the life of your fresh truffles by freezing, but I recommend you follow these instructions:

Pack the truffles in a shallow paper or cardboard box padded with tissue paper, both under and on top of the truffles. Double-wrap the box in plastic wrap, then place it in a zippered freezer bag, removing as much air as possible from the bag before sealing. Place the truffles in your refrigerator overnight. The next day, move to the freezer. When you are ready to enjoy your chocolates, let the truffles thaw in the refrigerator overnight. The next day, allow the truffles to sit at room temperature in the sealed freezer bag for 24 hours. Only when the truffles have fully thawed and come to room temperature should you remove them from their airtight packaging.

Sexy Mexi Truffles

The combination of chilies and chocolate is truly magical. More smoky and sweet than spicy, this truffle is redolent with warm flavors that call forth the scents and sunshine of warmer climes. Because I wanted to create a truffle that was as sexy in texture as it was in flavor, I have used whole spices and strained them out, rather than mixing their powdered versions. The result is a super-creamy, satiny-smooth ganache that I have to force myself not to just slurp up with a spoon. MAKES **64** TRUFFLES

1 CUP HEAVY CREAM, PLUS MORE AS NEEDED

1 WHOLE ANCHO CHILI POD, DE-STEMMED, DE-VEINED AND SEEDS REMOVED

1 CINNAMON STICK

1 WHOLE CARDAMOM POD

½ VANILLA BEAN

15 OUNCES BITTERSWEET CHOCOLATE

2 OUNCES INVERT SUGAR (SEE PAGE 36) OR MILD HONEY

5 TABLESPOONS VERY SOFT UNSALTED BUTTER

2 POUNDS MILK CHOCOLATE

Place the heavy cream in a medium saucepan. Tear the chili pod into pieces and toss it in with the cream. Crush the cinnamon stick and the cardamom pod with a kitchen mallet or in a mortar. Split the vanilla bean lengthwise and scrape out the seeds. Throw it all into the cream.

Heat the cream until it just begins to boil, give it a stir, then remove the pan from the heat. Cover and allow the cream to steep for an hour or more.

In the meantime, chop 12 ounces of the bittersweet chocolate and place it in a food processor. Pour the invert sugar or honey on top of it.

Strain the cream into a clean bowl, pressing on the solids to extract as much flavor as possible. If necessary, add a little more cream so that the flavored batch measures ¾ cup. Pour the cream back in the pan and heat it to a full boil.

Once the cream boils, pour it immediately over the chopped chocolate. Allow the cream to sit for a minute or two, then process the mixture for about 30 seconds. Add the butter in small chunks, then whir until the mixture is completely smooth and falls in thick blobs. It should have the consistency of pudding. Do not over-process, or your ganache will separate.

Scrape the emulsified ganache into a plastic-wrap–lined 8"x8" brownie pan. Level the ganache carefully with an offset icing spatula, spreading it all the way to the sides and completely into the corners. Allow the ganache to set at a cool room temperature (or in the refrigerator if your house is very warm) overnight.

When the ganache is set, and you are ready to finish your truffles, chop the remaining 2 pounds of chocolate, and melt and temper it (see pages 28–30). Remove the ganache from the pan by lifting it out by the plastic wrap. "Bottom" your ganache by spreading a very thin layer of tempered chocolate on the entire top surface of the ganache. When the chocolate has set, turn the slab over (so that the layer of chocolate is on the bottom) and cut it into 1" squares.

Dip the squares, chocolate side down, into the tempered chocolate using a dipping fork (see page 31). Alternatively, skip the "bottoming" step and roll the ganache, instead, into walnut-size balls and dip or decorate as desired (see pages 30–31).

To make your truffles look like the ones in the photograph, melt and temper the remaining 3 ounces of bittersweet chocolate (see pages 28–30). Spoon the tempered chocolate into a parchment decorating cone, cut the tip of the cone to create a tiny opening, and pipe two thin stripes of chocolate onto each truffle.

Earl Grey Truffles

When I was in college, my roommate Anne used to drink Earl Grey tea sweetened with honey and lightened with whole milk while we studied in the afternoon. This recipe is my attempt to recreate those flavors in a confection. MAKES 64 TRUFFLES

....

1 CUP HEAVY CREAM, PLUS MORE AS NEEDED

2 TABLESPOONS EARL GREY TEA LEAVES, SUCH AS TWINING'S

13 OUNCES MILK CHOCOLATE

1 OUNCE MILD HONEY

2 POUNDS BITTERSWEET CHOCOLATE

....

Place the heavy cream in a medium saucepan and bring to a near boil. Remove from heat, add the tea leaves, and cover. Allow the cream to steep for 5 minutes.

Chop the milk chocolate and place it in a food processor. Pour the honey on top of it.

Strain the cream into a glass measuring cup, pressing on the leaves to extract as much flavor as possible. If necessary, add cream so that the flavored batch measures ½ cup. Pour the cream back in the pan and heat until the mixture comes to a full boil.

Once the cream boils, pour immediately over the chopped chocolate. Allow the cream to sit for a minute or two, then process the mixture until it is completely smooth and falls in thick blobs; it should be the consistency of pudding. Do not over-process, or your ganache will separate.

Scrape the emulsified ganache into a plastic-wrap–lined 8"x8" brownie pan. Level the ganache carefully with an offset icing spatula, spreading it all the way to the sides and completely into the corners. Allow the ganache to set at a cool room temperature (or in the refrigerator if your house is very warm) overnight.

When the ganache is set, chop, then melt and temper the 2 pounds of bittersweet chocolate (see page 28–30). Remove the ganache from the pan by lifting it out by the plastic wrap. "Bottom" your ganache by spreading a very thin layer of tempered chocolate on the entire top surface of the ganache. When the chocolate has set, turn the slab over (so that the layer of chocolate is on the bottom) and cut it into 1" squares.

Dip the squares, chocolate side down, into the tempered chocolate using a dipping fork (see page 31). Alternatively, skip the "bottoming" step and roll the ganache, instead, into walnut-size balls and dip or decorate as desired (see pages 30–31).

Wild Raspberry Truffles

I'm not sure if there is any more perfect pairing than dark chocolate and raspberry. Dark chocolate's heavy, earthy overtones take flight when brightened by the racy, zingy flavors of super-tart fruits—raspberry being queen among them. Many raspberry truffle recipes call for raspberry extract or raspberry liqueur, but I always felt that using these types of flavorings made the final product just taste boozy, and a little cloying. If you concentrate a fresh raspberry puree, you will be rewarded with a burst of real raspberry flavor that leaves you wanting more, rather than the itch to go brush your teeth. MAKES 64 TRUFFLES

2¾ POUNDS BITTERSWEET CHOCOLATE

2 OUNCES INVERT SUGAR OR MILD HONEY

¼ CUP PLUS 2 TABLESPOONS HEAVY CREAM

¼ CUP PLUS 2 TABLESPOONS RASPBERRY PUREE (SEE PAGE 36)

5 TABLESPOONS VERY SOFT UNSALTED BUTTER

Chop 12 ounces of the chocolate and place it in a food processor. Pour the invert sugar or honey on top of the chocolate.

Combine the cream and raspberry puree in a small saucepan and bring to full boil over medium heat.

Once the cream boils, pour it immediately over the chopped chocolate. Allow the cream to sit for a minute or two, then process the mixture for about 30 seconds. Add the butter in small spoonfuls, then whir until the mixture is completely smooth and falls in thick blobs; it should be the consistency of pudding. Do not over-process, or your ganache will separate.

Scrape the emulsified ganache into a plastic-wrap–lined 8"x8" brownie pan. Level the ganache carefully with an offset icing spatula, spreading it all the way to the sides and completely into the corners. Allow the ganache to set at a cool room temperature (or in the refrigerator if your house is very warm) overnight.

Chop, then melt and temper the remaining 2 pounds of bittersweet chocolate (see page 28–30). Remove the ganache from the pan by lifting it out by the plastic wrap. "Bottom" your ganache by spreading a very thin layer of tempered chocolate on the entire top surface of the ganache. When the chocolate has set, turn the slab over and cut it into 1" squares.

Dip the squares, chocolate side down, into the tempered chocolate using a dipping fork (see page 31). Alternatively, skip the "bottoming" step and roll the ganache, instead, into walnut-size balls and dip or decorate as desired (see pages 30–31).

LOBSTER FOR CHOCOLATE

Here's the question I am most frequently asked by visitors, patrons, reporters, and friends: Why the hell did you decide to try making chocolate on a tiny little island in the middle of nowhere?

My answer is simple: I make beautiful, delicious chocolate in the place that I live because I can. There's not much I know how to do, but I feel very lucky that this thing—this trivial, extraneous, luxury item—is something that people value.

And I guess, for me, that's what work is all about. Putting something out there—a service, a product, a gift—that people value enough to give something in return. I feel like sometimes this very basic exchange of goods and services gets lost in our scramble to get noticed, to win more customers, in a world where we all have decreasing attention spans. Even our values become marketing opportunities: fair trade, sustainably grown, locally produced. What matters is how you package yourself, how efficiently, and with how much flash. I can't tell you how many times "experts" have told me that quality isn't even half of what makes up the value of a product. The rest is where you are, who you know, what color ribbon you use, what certifications you have.

Not that I'm against this. Let's face it, I'm no purist, no Luddite, and I admit that I do like the spotlight at times.

But mostly, I see my chocolate as a commodity. Something I make, that I can, in turn, exchange for something else of value. And sometimes it takes a twelve-year-old kid to remind me of that.

The other day I ran into Ethan Mao and his mom, Kate. Ethan hauls a string of traps from his skiff all summer for spending money. He asked me if I would consider trading chocolate for lobster later in the summer. I'm not sure that I've felt prouder of my product than I did at that moment. More than money, more than any ad or brochure or picture could communicate; all of the sudden my chocolate had a value that I could understand. This is why I do what I do in the place I call home. Because I can.

Hazelnut Coffee Truffles

I will confess to a small weakness for hazelnut-flavored coffees. And while I don't use the flavored stuff to make these truffles, all the things I love about these two ingredients shows up here: smooth and crunchy, sweet and bitter. **MAKES 64 TRUFFLES**

....

¾ CUP HEAVY CREAM

¼ CUP WHOLE ORGANIC COFFEE BEANS

2 POUNDS, 6 OUNCES MILK CHOCOLATE

7 OUNCES BITTERSWEET CHOCOLATE

6 OUNCES WHOLE, BLANCHED HAZELNUTS

2 TABLESPOONS VERY SOFT UNSALTED BUTTER

1 OUNCE INVERT SUGAR (PAGE 36) OR MILD HONEY

....

Place the heavy cream in a medium saucepan and bring to a near boil. Remove from heat, add the coffee beans, and cover. Allow the cream to steep for at least an hour.

While the cream is steeping, pre-heat your oven to 350 degrees and spread the hazelnuts on a cookie sheet. Roast the hazelnuts for 10 to 12 minutes, or until they just start to brown. Remove the hazelnuts from the oven, and set aside 4 ounces and allow them to cool completely. Place the remaining 2 ounces of hazelnuts in a food processor and grind them until they are almost paste-like. Add the butter and the invert sugar or the honey to the hazelnuts in the food processor and whir until you have a creamy paste that is speckled with small bits of hazelnut. Scrape this mixture into a small bowl and set aside. No need to wash the food processor bowl.

Chop the bittersweet chocolate and 6 ounces of the milk chocolate and place them both in the food processor.

Next, strain the steeped cream into a glass measuring cup, pressing on the beans to extract as much flavor as possible. If necessary, add a bit more cream so that the flavored batch measures ½ cup. Pour the cream back in the pan and heat it until the mixture comes to a full boil.

Once the cream boils, pour it immediately over the chopped chocolate. Allow the cream to sit for a minute or two, then process the mixture for about 30 seconds. Scrape in the hazelnut mixture and process until the ganache is completely smooth and falls in thick blobs; it should be the consistency of pudding. Do not over-process, or your ganache will separate.

Scrape the emulsified ganache into a plastic-wrap–lined 8"x8" brownie pan. Level the ganache carefully with an offset icing spatula, spreading it all the way to the sides and completely into the corners. Allow the ganache to set at a cool room temperature (or in the refrigerator if your house is very warm) overnight.

When the ganache is set, and you are ready to finish your truffles, melt and temper the remaining 2 pounds of milk chocolate (see pages 28–30). Remove the ganache from the pan by lifting it out by the plastic wrap. "Bottom" your ganache by spreading a very thin layer of tempered chocolate on the entire top surface of the ganache. When the chocolate has set, turn the slab over (so that the layer of chocolate is on the bottom) and cut it into 1" squares.

Press a whole hazelnut onto the top of each square, so that half of the nut is embedded in the ganache and half is emerging from the top.

Dip the squares, chocolate side down, into the tempered chocolate using a dipping fork (see page 31). Alternatively, skip the "bottoming" step and roll the ganache, instead, into walnut-size balls and dip (see pages 30–31). Chop the remaining hazelnuts and sprinkle on top of each finished truffle before the chocolate sets.

CHOCOLATE
for
BREAKFAST

Orange-Scented Chocolate-Espresso Cinnamon Buns

When I ran out of milk during a morning bake several years ago, I was forced to grab desperately for a substitution to make these buns. The carton of orange juice in the refrigerator seemed the only likely candidate at the time. And from that, this recipe evolved. **MAKES 8**

For the filling:

¾ CUP DARK BROWN SUGAR

¼ CUP GRANULATED SUGAR

2 TEASPOONS CINNAMON

⅛ TEASPOON GROUND CLOVES

⅛ TEASPOON SALT

2 TABLESPOONS UNSALTED BUTTER, MELTED

1 CUP CHOPPED BITTERSWEET CHOCOLATE

For the dough:

2½ CUPS FLOUR

1¼ TEASPOONS BAKING POWDER

½ TEASPOON BAKING SODA

½ TEASPOON SALT

½ CUP ORANGE JUICE

2 TABLESPOONS GRANULATED SUGAR

½ CUP BUTTERMILK

6 TABLESPOONS UNSALTED BUTTER, MELTED

1 TABLESPOON INSTANT ESPRESSO POWDER

For the icing:

3 OUNCES CREAM CHEESE

¼ CUP ORANGE JUICE CONCENTRATE, THAWED

FINELY GRATED ZEST OF ONE ORANGE

2 TABLESPOONS SUPERFINE SUGAR

Heat the oven to 425 degrees. Cut a large piece of parchment paper into roughly 8 4"x4" squares. Spray an 8-cup muffin tin lightly with cooking oil (if you don't have an 8-cup muffin tin, just use a 12-cup one).

In a medium-size bowl, make the filling. Stir together the brown sugar, the ¼ cup sugar, cinnamon, cloves, and salt. Stir in 2 tablespoons of the melted butter, until the mixture feels a little damp. Mix in the chocolate.

To make the dough, in a large bowl, whisk together the flour, baking powder, baking soda, salt and sugar.

In a large glass measuring cup, stir together the buttermilk, orange juice, melted butter, and espresso powder.

Pour this mixture into the flour mixture and stir until a shaggy dough forms. Don't overmix. Turn out onto a lightly floured board and pat into a rectangle, about ½ inch thick, with the long sides facing you.

Spread the filling mixture onto the entire surface of your rectangle and pat it down lightly. Scatter the chopped chocolate over the filling.

Working from the side closest to you, roll up the dough jelly-roll fashion. Cut this log into 8 discs.

Place a 4"x4" square of parchment paper on top of one of the cavities of your muffin tin, and then place a disc of dough, cut side up, onto the square and gently push the roll, paper and all, into the muffin cavity. Repeat this step with each roll.

Bake for 20 to 25 minutes. Remove the buns from the oven and allow to cool slightly.

While the buns are baking, whir the cream cheese, orange juice concentrate, orange zest, and superfine sugar in a food processor, until the mixture is completely smooth. Frost the buns with thick blobs of icing and serve warm.

ORANGE-
SCENTED
CHOCOLATE-
ESPRESSO
CINNAMON
BUNS,
PAGES 52–53

Bittersweet Chocolate Chunk and Cream Cheese Scones

I know I'm not supposed to say things like I'm going to say right now: There are no better scones on the planet than those made by Kyra Alex at Lily's Café across the water from us in Stonington. They are truly magical, so if you ever find yourself in the neighborhood (perhaps next summer on your way to the Isle au Haut mailboat to come see us), you simply must stop at Lily's. She makes other good stuff, too (her Cold Chinese Noodles, and a tuna melt to die for), but the scones, well, I've already said it.

That said, the following recipe—developed in my kitchen over many, many years of trying to recreate something similar in texture to my favorites—ain't half bad. In fact, they've developed their own passionate following among certain of our cafe clientele.

The trick with this dough is not to overwork it. That may seem like a tall order when you see how dry and shaggy the dough is before you turn it out on the board. But all I can say is have faith. If you can manage to form it into a disc, get it cut, and transferred to the sheet pan without it completely falling apart, you will be rewarded with a gem of a scone.

MAKES 8

2 LARGE EGG YOLKS

1 CUP HEAVY CREAM

1 TEASPOON VANILLA EXTRACT

3 CUPS FLOUR

½ CUP GRANULATED SUGAR

4 TEASPOONS BAKING POWDER

½ TEASPOON BAKING SODA

½ TEASPOON SEA SALT

8 TABLESPOONS UNSALTED BUTTER, COLD

4 OUNCES CREAM CHEESE, COLD

1 CUP CHOPPED BITTERSWEET CHOCOLATE

Preheat the oven to 400 degrees.

In a glass measuring cup, whisk together the egg yolks and enough heavy cream to measure 1 cup. Stir in the vanilla extract. Set aside.

In a large mixing bowl, whisk together the flour, sugar, baking powder, baking soda, and salt.

Grate the butter directly into the dry ingredients, and mix in with your hands, rubbing gently.

Cut or tear the cream cheese into small chunks, and toss into the dry ingredients. Toss in the chocolate, and stir it all together.

Pour in the egg mixture and mix quickly with a large rubber spatula. Add more cream if needed, stirring briskly, with a few strokes after any addition. You should have a crumbly mixture that barely qualifies as dough at this point.

Turn the dough onto a cutting board and quickly knead together using a bench scraper to help you form the chunky mixture into a dough that barely holds together. Flatten the dough into a disc and cut into 8 triangles with a very sharp knife. Place the triangles onto two parchment-lined cookie sheets, four to a sheet, and sprinkle the tops with sugar.

Bake for 20 to 25 minutes. Rotate the sheets once during baking. The scones are done when they are lightly browned and just firm to the touch.

VARIATION: Replace the chocolate with 1 cup of frozen Maine blueberries. You may need to increase cooking time a little.

Ricotta Doughnut Holes with Orange-Scented Dipping Chocolate

Steve and I spent most of 2006, the year before we opened Black Dinah Chocolatiers, researching the chocolate industry and trying to make ends meet. I was no longer employed by the Keeper's House, and we still had a lot of work to do on our business plan and product line. So, Steve spent the summer earning our 'capital' by hiring himself out as a house painter and carpenter, and I sent flyers to everyone on the island that I was now available for private catering events.

As a side job, Steve and I dug a long-forgotten old children's playhouse out of the woods, and after subjecting it to a few minor renovations, set it in a little grassy patch where our long driveway meets the island's main road.

Every morning, I would stock the little stand with cinnamon rolls, cakes, muffins, cookies, and pies. On Sundays I baked bread. And on Saturdays I made doughnuts. I set out a large thermos of coffee, a few paper cups, and jars of sugar and cream. We stocked an ice chest full of bottled water and natural soda and put that out there, too. Steve found an old wooden folding chair at one of his project sites, and we set that up next to the stand, along with a copy of yesterday's paper. On the ground, next to the chair, we placed an inconspicuous coffee can: the universal symbol for the honor system. It was our very first café.

Though these days, our café is just a little farther down the driveway, the menu is much the same, and includes chairs to sit in and a copy of yesterday's paper. And we still offer doughnuts on Saturdays. MAKES ROUGHLY 30 TINY DOUGHNUTS

. . . .

For the dipping chocolate:

¼ CUP BITTERSWEET CHOCOLATE, CHOPPED

¼ CUP Dutch-process COCOA

1 CUP WHOLE MILK

½ CUP STRONG BREWED COFFEE

2 TABLESPOONS GRANULATED SUGAR

⅛ TEASPOON FRESHLY GRATED ORANGE ZEST

. . . .

For the doughnuts:

1 CUP WHOLE-MILK RICOTTA CHEESE

2 LARGE EGGS, AT ROOM TEMPERATURE

½ CUP FLOUR

1 ½ TEASPOONS BAKING POWDER

⅛ TEASPOON SALT

⅛ TEASPOON GROUND GINGER

¼ TEASPOON FRESHLY GROUND NUTMEG

¼ TEASPOON CINNAMON

1 TABLESPOON HONEY

½ TEASPOON VANILLA EXTRACT

SAFFLOWER OIL, FOR FRYING

CONFECTIONERS' SUGAR, FOR DUSTING

· ·

Place the chopped chocolate, cocoa, milk, coffee, sugar, and zest in a medium bowl, and set the bowl over a pot of simmering water. Allow the ingredients to melt together while you make the doughnuts.

To make the doughnuts, combine the ricotta and eggs in a large bowl. Beat in the flour, baking powder, salt, ginger, nutmeg, cinnamon, honey, and vanilla extract. Mix to form a smooth batter.

Pour 2 or 3 inches of oil into a cast-iron pot, and heat to 370 degrees. Drop the batter by teaspoonfuls into the hot oil, turning after a minute or so. Cook for another minute and then transfer to a pan lined with paper towels. Continue until you have fried all the batter.

After you have fried the doughnuts, whisk together the dipping chocolate ingredients until the sauce is smooth. If there are still some lumps, gently re-heat and whisk again over the simmering water.

Serve the doughnuts, four or five to a person, on dessert plates, and dust with confectioners' sugar. Accompany each plate with a small bowl of dipping chocolate.

Banana-Coconut Chocolate Swirl Bread

You can make this with or without the coconut; with or without the chocolate swirl. Very versatile, but always delicious. MAKES 1 LOAF

1½ CUPS FLOUR

1½ TEASPOONS BAKING SODA

½ TEASPOON SALT

8 TABLESPOONS UNSALTED BUTTER, AT ROOM TEMPERATURE

2 TABLESPOONS COCONUT OIL OR OLIVE OIL

½ CUP GRANULATED SUGAR

½ CUP DARK BROWN SUGAR

2 LARGE EGGS, AT ROOM TEMPERATURE

1 TEASPOON VANILLA EXTRACT

3 OR 4 RIPE BANANAS, MASHED

1 CUP UNSWEETENED SMALL SHRED COCONUT

4 OUNCES BITTERSWEET CHOCOLATE, MELTED

Grease a 9" loaf pan and heat the oven to 350 degrees.

In a medium-size bowl, whisk together the flour, baking soda, and salt. Set aside.

In the bowl of a stand mixer, cream together the butter, coconut oil, and sugars until the mixture looks light in color. Beat in the eggs, one at a time, then add the vanilla. Stir in the bananas.

Beat in the flour mixture until all the ingredients are just blended.

Remove 1 cup of this batter to a small bowl. Stir the melted chocolate into the smaller amount of batter until well blended.

Stir the coconut into the larger amount of batter.

Pour the coconut batter into the prepared loaf pan. Glop the chocolate batter by spoonfuls on top of the coconut batter. With a butter knife, swirl the two batters together, making sure to cut all the way down to the bottom of the loaf pan. Sprinkle the top of the batter with a little extra coconut.

Bake for 45 to 60 minutes, until a toothpick pricked into the center comes away with just a few small crumbs.

Cool the bread for 10 minutes, then release onto a rack and cool completely. This bread freezes beautifully if wrapped in a double layer of plastic wrap.

Chocolate Gingerbread Pancakes

I decided long ago that morning was the best time to eat chocolate. Guests at the Keeper's House would come shuffling down the stairs in search of their morning coffee and often find me enjoying a slice of last night's chocolate cake while I cooked their omelets and pancakes. I like those things too, but there is nothing like a bit of chocolate in the morning to start the day off right.

In an effort to make this practice a little more socially acceptable, I came up with this recipe. I like the pancakes dressed with a dollop of sour cream and a generous drizzle of warm maple syrup. Oh, and yes, they taste amazing with a few slices of crispy bacon.

MAKES ROUGHLY 16

....

2 CUPS FLOUR

1 TABLESPOON BAKING POWDER

1 TEASPOON CINNAMON

1 TEASPOON GROUND GINGER

⅛ TEASPOON GROUND CLOVES

1 TEASPOON SALT

2 LARGE EGGS, AT ROOM TEMPERATURE

2 CUPS BUTTERMILK

3 TABLESPOONS BUTTER, MELTED, PLUS MORE FOR THE SKILLET

¼ CUP MOLASSES

2 TABLESPOONS DARK BROWN SUGAR

2 OUNCES BITTERSWEET CHOCOLATE, MELTED AND COOLED

....

In a medium-size bowl, whisk together the flour, baking powder, cinnamon, ginger, cloves, and salt.

Separate the eggs, placing the whites in a medium-size metal bowl. Mix the yolks with the buttermilk, melted butter, molasses, and brown sugar. Stir in the melted chocolate.

Beat the whites until they hold stiff (but not dry) peaks.

Stir the yolk mixture into the flour mixture and mix thoroughly (use a whisk if necessary, to get rid of most of the lumps). Fold in the whites.

Heat a large skillet over a medium flame. Melt a little butter in the skillet and swirl it around so that it covers the entire surface of the pan.

When the skillet is hot, drop the batter by ¼ cupfuls, and cook until the batter is bubbly

and just beginning to dry along the edges. Flip the pancakes, cover the pan, and cook for another few minutes, or until the center of a pancake springs back when poked with your finger.

Keep the cakes warm on a cookie sheet in the oven while you cook up the rest of the batter.

VARIATION:
Chocolate Gingerbread-Bacon Waffles

Cook up eights slices of thick-cut bacon. Remove to paper towels, cool, and then crumble the bacon into small pieces.

Follow the recipe and instructions for the pancakes, but add 2 tablespoons of bacon fat to the liquid ingredients.

Before you fold in the egg whites, stir in the crumbled bacon.

Cook on a waffle iron, according to the manufacturer's directions. Serve with butter and warmed maple syrup.

TARTS, PIES,
and
CAKES

Peruvian Chocolate Tart with Raspberry Curd

During the 2010 café season, we were very lucky to host a weekly Sunday concert with cellist Jake Woolen. Jake would begin playing at noon, and we would offer a lunch special and an over-the-top dessert to the after-church crowd that attended. When I came up with this recipe, I thought it would go great with cello music. Seriously. Which is how I tested it—over the kitchen sink, with Jake's sublime playing wafting in from the café. And to this day, it is still the best thing I have ever put in my mouth.

But then again, it could have been the cello music. SERVES 8 TO 10

For the curd:

4 LARGE EGG YOLKS

½ CUP RASPBERRY PUREE (SEE PAGE 36)

1 TEASPOON LEMON JUICE

1 CUP GRANULATED SUGAR

⅛ TEASPOON SALT

6 TABLESPOONS UNSALTED BUTTER

For the crust:

¼ CUP GRANULATED SUGAR

¼ TEASPOON SALT

1 TEASPOON VANILLA

8 TABLESPOONS UNSALTED BUTTER, MELTED

1 CUP FLOUR

For the filling:

8 OUNCES PERUVIAN CHOCOLATE (OR ANY GOOD-QUALITY
   BITTERSWEET CHOCOLATE), CHOPPED

1 CUP HALF AND HALF

¼ CUP RASPBERRY PUREE

1 LARGE EGG, LIGHTLY BEATEN

To make the curd, stir together the egg yolks, raspberry puree, lemon juice, sugar, and salt into a medium-size bowl. Place the bowl over a pot of simmering water careful to make sure the bowl doesn't touch the water. Cut the butter into small pieces and add it to the bowl. Whisk or stir the mixture until it thickens and keeps a soft shape as it falls from your whisk or spoon, about 20 minutes. Try not to boil it, otherwise you'll get scrambled eggs in raspberry juice.

Remove the curd from the heat and pour it into a small bowl. Place a sheet of plastic wrap directly on the surface of the curd. Cool completely.

Preheat the oven to 350 degrees.

To make the crust, combine the sugar, salt, and vanilla in a small bowl. Pour in the melted butter, then mix in the flour. Press the resulting soft dough along the bottom and completely up the sides of a 9" tart pan. Place the pan on a cookie sheet and bake for 20 minutes, or until the crust just barely begins to brown. Remove the tart shell from the oven, but keep the oven on.

Meanwhile, make the filling. Place the chopped chocolate into a medium-size bowl. Pour the half and half into a small saucepan and bring it to a full boil. Remove the pan from the heat and immediately pour it all at once onto the chocolate. Stir or whisk until completely smooth. Whisk in the raspberry puree, then whisk in the egg.

Pour this mixture into the hot crust and return it to the oven. Bake for another 10 minutes, or until the filling has begun to set around the edges but still wiggles a little in the middle. Remove the tart from the oven and cool completely.

When both the curd and the tart are completely cool, spoon the curd onto the top of the tart, spreading it out to the edges of the tart filling (your crust will be showing). Chill the tart for several hours before serving. Decorate with a few turbans of piped whipped cream, or a handful of fresh mint leaves.

Chocolate Meringue Pie

Lisa Turner, who is not only a wonderful cook and a generous soul, but also a good listener, wanted to make our friend Albert a very special birthday dessert. Albert had often bemoaned the fact that the last place he could ask for a slice of chocolate meringue pie, and have anyone know what he was talking about, was long ago in his home state of Tennessee. Now, Lisa is famous for her lemon meringue pie, which is known to go for $500 or more at the annual school pie auction. The reason for the pie's fame is the sheer shock value of the meringue on top. "Eleven egg whites," Lisa explains to the stunned auction audience every year.

When Lisa called to get my recipe for Bittersweet Chocolate Pudding to use as a filling for Albert's Chocolate Meringue Pie, I was dubious. The pudding is rich and fine, and I couldn't imagine it topped with anything other than lightly whipped, subtly sweetened heavy cream.

But, as it turned out, Lisa's ginormous, gloriously sweet, perfectly browned meringue ended up being the perfect foil for the soft, bitter denseness of the pudding it engulfed. Add a spectacularly flaky all-butter crust, and Albert had himself a new birthday tradition—and Lisa had an enormously successful recipe. SERVES 8 TO 10

....

For the filling:

1 RECIPE OF BITTERSWEET CHOCOLATE PUDDING (PAGE 107)

....

For the crust:

1 CUP PLUS 2 TABLESPOONS FLOUR

½ TEASPOON SALT

1 TEASPOON GRANULATED SUGAR

8 OUNCES UNSALTED BUTTER, VERY COLD

3 TO 4 TABLESPOONS COLD WATER

....

For the meringue:

6 LARGE EGG WHITES, AT ROOM TEMPERATURE

⅔ CUP GRANULATED SUGAR

Prepare and thoroughly chill the Bittersweet Chocolate Pudding.

To make the crust, combine the flour, salt, and sugar in a large bowl. Grate the butter directly into the flour mixture and mix in quickly with your hands.

Stir in 3 tablespoons of the water, but don't mix too thoroughly. Mix in more water until you have a rough shaggy mass of flour and dough.

Turn this out onto an unfloured cutting board (or a stone slab), and gently—but quickly—work the dough together by alternatively smearing out with the heel of your hand and scraping it up with a bench scraper. When the dough holds together, immediately roll it out on a heavily floured cutting board, place it in your pie plate, and crimp the edges.

Prick the crust all over with a fork, wrap in plastic, and freeze.

When the crust is frozen, preheat your oven to 400 degrees, unwrap the crust, and line it with aluminum foil. Fill the crust to the brim with dried beans and bake for 20 to 25 minutes, or until the crust is golden brown. Cool the crust completely, and remove the foil and beans.

Turn the oven down to 300 degrees.

Place the egg whites in the bowl of a stand mixer and beat with the whisk attachment until the whites hold soft peaks. While the mixer is going, pour in the sugar very slowly. Beat until the peaks are stiff and glossy, but not dry or grainy.

Remove the pudding from the refrigerator and scoop it into the crust, leveling it off with an offset icing spatula.

Spread the meringue over the entire surface of the pie, making sure that it makes contact with the crust along the entire edge. This will help prevent the meringue from shrinking during baking.

Place the pie in the oven and bake for 20 to 30 minutes, until the meringue is golden and cooked through. Remove from the oven and cool. Chill the pie for 6 to 8 hours before serving.

Pumpkin Cheesecake with Elderberry Glaze and Chocolate Walnut Crumb Crust

Confession: I am a life-long despiser of pumpkin pie. The only thing that would make me any less American is if I hated apple pie and baseball. Fortunately, I love apple pie, and, honestly, I don't know enough about baseball to either love or hate it. But pumpkin pie? I just can't get into it. And believe me, I've tried.

But I adore pumpkin. And Thanksgiving, *the* pumpkin pie holiday, is my favorite holiday of the year.

For the past five years, we've had a rotating Thanksgiving dinner on the island. Whoever hosts is responsible for the turkey, but beyond that, the dinner is a structured potluck, where guests bring the dishes that either are their specialty, or which define the holiday for them. Diana Santospago, the local innkeeper, always volunteers to help with the decorations, and the host house is transformed into a glittering cornucopia of apples, bittersweet, candles, and gourds.

Usually, as long as there's plenty of stuffing and gravy, I'm good. But this particular year, I got it into my head that I had to have a pumpkin dessert. So I volunteered to make the pie.

Needless to say, there was a lot of grumbling when, at dessert time, everyone realized that the pumpkin pie wasn't a pie at all, but a cheesecake. Then we all took our first bite. And just like that, we had a new Thanksgiving tradition.

If you're not lucky enough to know someone like islander Kathie Fiveash, who makes elderberry jelly from her garden, and you can't find it in your local grocery, feel free to substitute black currant—or even blueberry—jelly. SERVES 10 TO 12

....

For the crust:

1 ¼ CUPS CHOCOLATE WAFER CRUMBS (IF I DON'T HAVE HOMEMADE
   FROM THE CAFÉ ON HAND, I USE NABISCO)

⅓ CUP FINELY GROUND WALNUTS

5 TABLESPOONS UNSALTED BUTTER, MELTED

¼ CUP GRANULATED SUGAR

....

For the filling and glaze:

1 POUND PUMPKIN PUREE (SEE PAGE 36) OR CANNED PUMPKIN

1 ½ POUNDS CREAM CHEESE

1 CUP GRANULATED SUGAR

½ TEASPOON CINNAMON

¼ TEASPOON NUTMEG

¼ TEASPOON GROUND GINGER

6 LARGE EGGS

2 TABLESPOONS LEMON JUICE

½-PINT JAR ELDERBERRY JELLY

....

Preheat the oven to 350 degrees, and grease a 9" springform pan with butter. Place ¼ cup of the wafer crumbs in the pan and coat the entire inside of the pan, using the same method as you would to flour a buttered cake pan. Wrap the entire outside of the pan in several layers of commercial-quality plastic wrap.

Place the remaining 1 cup of chocolate wafer crumbs (and any excess from the pan), walnuts, melted butter, and sugar in a medium-size bowl and mix thoroughly. Press this mixture onto the bottom of the pan.

Next, make the filling. In a food processor, blend the pumpkin and cream cheese until smooth. Add the sugar, cinnamon, nutmeg, and ginger, and process. Add the eggs, two at a time, processing until smooth after each addition. Finally, mix in the lemon juice. Scrape this filling into the pan, level the top with an offset spatula, place the springform into a roasting pan large enough to hold it, and then pour boiling water into the roasting pan so that it comes halfway up the springform.

Bake for 1½ to 2 hours, removing the pan from the oven when there is just a small wiggly area in the middle.

Take the pan out of the water, and allow it to cool completely on a rack. Chill the cheesecake thoroughly.

When you are ready to serve it, remove it from the refrigerator and release the sides of the pan. Heat the elderberry jam gently in a small saucepan over a low flame. The point is not to heat it up, but to warm it enough that it becomes liquid. Pour the resulting glaze over the entire top of the cheesecake, leveling it out with an offset icing spatula.

Chickens, Hawks, and French Chocolate

There are lots of things about my life that, in any given moment, make me take a step back, shake my head, and wonder—sometimes audibly and with expletives—how I ever got to be here. You'd think they'd get less so the older I get, but that doesn't seem to be the case. Thank god for that, really, that life—and often the little things in it—still inspire, awe, and wonder.

When you get right down to it, I can't deny that if I were still living in, say, Santa Cruz, I might not feel this way as often as I do living on the island. Moving to Maine happened largely by accident; I fell in love with a man who wanted to be here. It was never on my list of places to live, much less visit. Paris, Athens, Ireland, Venezuela, Argentina: yes. Maine; not so much. But you should try it sometime; dump a born and bred suburban California girl in rural Maine and see what happens. Sure, she speaks the same language, but the culture shock couldn't be any more dramatic than if it were another country.

Of course, it's been almost eleven years now—six since we moved to the island. So the culture shock has long worn off—but not the magic of falling in love with a place and its people that inspired me to stay in the first place. The little things that I mentioned before—the ones that inspire awe and wonder, the ones that challenge my beliefs, my upbringing, my education, the ones that aren't just magical unto themselves, but magical also because I have a role in them—they still happen all the time.

This past Tuesday, after a wild day of running errands on the mainland, I returned home on the afternoon mailboat, loaded up the truck with my purchases, which included several shipments of French chocolate that arrived on the dock earlier that day, and, instead of going straight home, drove to Albert and Kathie's house where I had a date with their chickens. Albert and Kathie, who were away visiting friends in Boston and had asked me to feed and collect eggs for a few days, live on the east side of the island.

That people as normal as Albert and Kathie live in the spot that they do never ceases to amaze me. And I mean normal, like I'm normal. Regular people who work for a living. Albert bartered for this land in the 60's, and built the house here with his own hands. The floor to ceiling windows flood the entire first floor with light and celebrate the sweeping view of the eastern shore of the island, the sea, and the islands beyond. At today's price of real estate, even with it taking a dive, the chicken coop here is probably worth a million bucks.

So taking care of these chickens is no big hardship. I come, change the water, make sure they have food, and collect the eggs. I don't even have to break ice out of the water because it sits on top of its own little heater. How cool is that? The only real challenge is Kathie's pain-in-the-ass rooster, Hawkeye. He's aggressive and cranky and beligerent. In the spring he has an insatiable libido, endured heroically by the ten hens he lives with. My arrival at the house is usually trumpeted by his crowing, and he doesn't stop until I leave. When I enter the chicken house, he stays inside to guard while the hens scatter out into the yard. He pecks and crows and fiercely guards the nests. He is thoroughly unloveable, and to some degree I dread facing him.

And so it's surprising that when I got out of the truck on Tuesday I didn't notice that Hawkeye *wasn't* crowing. It wasn't until I stepped into the chicken house and found the hens huddled in the corner—and not racing for the door—that it occurred to me that it was strangely quiet. I looked for Hawkeye in the pile of softly clucking birds and couldn't find his plume of iridescent green feathers. And why weren't the hens leaving? Usually they're so spooked by me that they can't get out into the yard fast enough. And then it occurred to me that the chickens weren't spooked, they were *terrified*. By something way scarier than me.

I barely had time to do a quick headcount when I heard terrorized squawking from the yard. I ran outside to find a young hawk pressing a fat, rust-colored hen into the spring mud. I banged on the fence and shouted at the hawk, who released the hen in surprise, flew to the end of the fenced yard, and promptly got tangled in the chicken wire. The hen high-tailed it back into the house, where I shut her and the rest of her sisters in.

And that's when I discovered him; right there where a small ramp leads up from the yard to the little door of the henhouse was the haughty telltale plume of the rooster's tail feathers—and a little beyond that, Hawkeye himself.

His head had been eaten, all of his neck and most of one wing. He lay in a magnificent pillow of glittering feathers, his body still warm and bleeding into the mud. I grasped him by one of his feet, carried him out of the chicken yard, and plopped him rather unceremoniously onto Albert and Kathie's front lawn. I still had the hawk to deal with.

Still tangled in the fence, the hawk was complaining in bravely subdued "scree screes" from the far side of the chicken yard. He was big, looked hurt, and sounded pissed. I stood there in my street clothes, hatless, gloveless, and thoroughly unprepared for this Wild Kingdom drama unfolding before me, and decided I definitely needed help.

The island has no law enforcement, no stoplights or signs, and no leash laws. We do, however, have an animal control officer. His name is Greg, and fifteen minutes after I hung up with his girlfriend Diana, they pulled up the drive in their truck.

There were no cages, no leather braces, no special gloves. Greg just simply walked into the chicken yard, untangled the bird from the fence, walked out, and after a few minutes of us admiring the fierce raptor up close, he let him go. The hawk spread his wings, circled dizzily for a few minutes, then found a perch in an island spruce where he, presumably, stopped to gather his wits before embarking on any additional predatory adventures.

After Greg and Diana left, I packed up Hawkeye in a few plastic Hannaford shopping bags and placed him in Kathie and Albert's refrigerator. He wouldn't be good eating, but I knew that Kathie would want to see her fallen soldier and give him a fitting goodbye. Because that's the kind of people they are.

And for as much as I disliked that bird, I couldn't help but feel that he did deserve the honor of a decent burial, and not to be scavenged unceremoniously by crows or coyotes. If he had no other purpose, that rooster lived to guard his flock. A noble death to die like that—claws out, screaming and fighting, doing the one job he was born to do—and in the end, ultimately, success.

I drove home, unpacked, and only then remembered the French chocolate I had ordered as a possible replacement for the Venezuelan stuff I've been having trouble getting. I usually don't dig into my chocolate as soon as it arrives, but something about the day—feathers and blood and mud on my street clothes, the thought of a torn, unplucked bird in my friends' refrigerator, a small death by violence—I just wanted to come in contact with something fine. First, an almost palpable wave of chocolate aroma…a small chunk in my hand, then smooth on my tongue, exquisite and utterly delicious. And, yes, fine. As fine as life.

White-Chocolate Lavender Pound Cake

The white chocolate and lavender serve very well here as rich undertones in this not-so-sweet, finely textured, crackly topped cake. Accompanied by a scoop of honey-sweetened ice cream, this is a dreamy dessert. When it comes to lavender in confections and baked goods, there is a very fine line between soapy and sublime. Even if you adore lavender, chances are the family and friends you are feeding your cakes or cookies to don't. So please, for the sake of the rest of us, remember that a little goes a long way.

Take note, too, that there is a big difference between culinary lavender and other kinds. I recommend a high-quality, organic English lavender. MAKES 1 LOAF

½ CUP MILK

1 TABLESPOON DRIED LAVENDER BLOSSOMS,
    CRUSHED WITH A MORTAR AND PESTLE, OR CHOPPED FINELY

1 VANILLA BEAN

8 TABLESPOONS BUTTER

¾ CUP GRANULATED SUGAR

1 ½ TEASPOONS BAKING POWDER

½ TEASPOON SALT

4 LARGE EGGS, AT ROOM TEMPERATURE

1 TEASPOON VANILLA EXTRACT

8 OUNCES WHITE CHOCOLATE, MELTED AND COOLED

2 CUPS FLOUR

Preheat the oven to 350 degrees, and lightly grease a 9" loaf pan.

Place the milk and the crushed lavender blossoms into a small saucepan. Split the vanilla bean lengthwise and scrape the seeds into the milk, tossing the pod in after it. Bring the milk to a boil, then remove from the heat and allow it to steep until it has cooled to room temperature. Pluck out the vanilla pod.

In a stand mixer (or by hand), cream the butter, sugar, baking powder, and salt. Add the eggs one at a time, mixing thoroughly and scraping the bowl after each addition. Mix in the milk and the teaspoon of vanilla extract, then pour in the white chocolate and mix until combined.

Add the flour all at once and beat the mixture thoroughly. The batter will be very thick.

Scrape the batter into the loaf pan and spread evenly.

Bake for 50 minutes to an hour. The cake is done when a toothpick inserted into its center comes out clean. Cool completely in the pan, then release and slice. The cake develops more flavor as it sits.

Olive Oil Chocolate Cake with Chocolate Buttercream

When people walk into the cafe and see this cake sitting in the pastry case, they always ask, "What is *that*?" "Chocolate cake," I answer simply, not quite sure what the big mystery is. It looks like a chocolate cake, smells like one, tastes like one. So much so, in fact, that I never thought to write a label for it. But people still ask, and then roll their eyes at my answer. Anyhoo, the cake is simple; the frosting a labor of love—but worth it.

SERVES 10 TO 12

....

For the cake:

½ CUP VEGETABLE OIL, SUCH AS SAFFLOWER

½ CUP GOOD-QUALITY OLIVE OIL

2 CUPS DARK BROWN SUGAR

3 LARGE EGGS, AT ROOM TEMPERATURE

2¼ CUPS FLOUR, SIFTED

½ CUP DUTCH-PROCESS COCOA, SIFTED

2 TEASPOONS BAKING SODA

½ TEASPOON SALT

½ CUP BUTTERMILK

1 CUP BOILING WATER

2 TEASPOONS VANILLA EXTRACT

....

For the buttercream frosting:

4 LARGE EGG WHITES AT ROOM TEMPERATURE

1 CUP GRANULATED SUGAR

2 CUPS (4 STICKS) UNSALTED BUTTER, AT ROOM TEMPERATURE

12 OUNCES BITTERSWEET CHOCOLATE, MELTED AND COOLED

....

Grease by hand, or spray with vegetable oil, two 9"x3" round cake pans. For best results, line the pans with parchment paper.

Preheat the oven to 375 degrees.

Combine vegetable and olive oils and sugar, and beat in a stand mixer until combined. Add the eggs and beat until light in color and the sugar has completely dissolved.

In a separate bowl, sift together the flour, cocoa, baking soda, and salt. Add the flour mixture and buttermilk alternately into the egg mixture.

In a heatproof measuring cup, stir together the boiling water and vanilla. With the beaters going, add the hot water to the cake batter in a slow, steady stream. Beat until fully incorporated.

Pour the batter into the pans and bake until the cake just begins to come away from the sides and is fully cooked in the middle, about 30 minutes. Cool the cakes completely in the pans, then release.

To make the frosting, beat the egg whites with a *very* clean whisk attachment in the *very* clean, grease-free bowl of your stand mixer (sometimes I'll douse a paper towel with a little rum or Kahlua and wipe down the inside of the bowl to make sure there is no residual oil on it from the last project). When the whites hold soft peaks, add the sugar in a slow steady stream. After all the sugar is added, beat until the whites hold stiff, glossy peaks.

Reduce the speed of the mixer somewhat, and start adding the butter in clumps of about 2 tablespoons each. Wait until the first clump is fully incorporated before adding the next. The whites will deflate the second you add the butter. At this point, stop the mixer very briefly and scrape the sides of the bowl so that all the whites are mixed in. If at any point the mixture starts looking curdled, stop adding butter, but keep beating. Just keep beating and it will eventually smooth out. I promise. Continue to beat in any remaining butter until it is all added. Remember: this is *butter*cream.

When all the butter has been added and the buttercream is perfectly smooth—silky and light as a cloud—scrape in your chocolate and mix thoroughly.

Spread the top of one cake layer thickly with the frosting. Top with the remaining layer and cover the entire cake with the frosting.

A BITTERSWEET BALANCE

Labor Day, the last day of summer, brought weather so fine I could practically taste it when I walked out in the morning to turn around the cafe sign. The wind was up, but it was a warm one, coaxing a smile—the kind that assaults the face when no one is watching, the corners of my mouth drawing my arms up in a delicious stretch, embracing the warm dry air, the late-summer sun.

I've been a news junkie lately. I get up in the morning, make the coffee, bring a cup up to Steve, and then start making cinnamon rolls. By the time I come-to, "Marketplace" is on the radio, the cinnamon rolls and the biscuit rolls are done, and the scones are in the oven. I'm halfway through mixing muffin batter and am planning the Italian meringue buttercream I'll make from the week's leftover egg whites. Mid-morning brings a hurricane crashing into the Gulf Coast and I think a chocolate cake is in order, layered thickly with the buttercream spiked with a good dose of Venezuelan chocolate—it's good for what ails us. All this sorrow and hope and tragedy. And recently, closer to home, island in-fighting that always seems to plague the end of summer, as if we were all peevish at its departure, dreading the dark months to come. But, as we well know from history, we cannot feed each other cake and expect our problems to disappear.

So, I spent the latter part of the afternoon catching a few tears with a dish towel, in an effort to keep them from seizing the chocolate I was tempering for lavender truffles. I hate watching my neighbors fight, stand by while misunderstandings turn to maelstroms, whirring and wailing into personal hurricanes crashing into the September-quiet shores of our own little coasts. I can't help but think of Tita crying into her sister's wedding cake batter in *Like Water for Chocolate*. What havoc that created—Gertrudis riding off naked with revolutionaries and Rosaura losing her son and later becoming sterile. All because of a few tears in the wrong place.

I hope those lavender truffles don't make people sad. Instead, I hope that they somehow communicate the complicated fabric of community life. Maybe not so literally, but somehow infusing our palates with compassion, a willingness to understand, forgive. Make the words off our tongues sweeter, lessen the bile, ease our frustrations, douse our anger with simple pleasure, fleeting joy; and a desire to seek joy rather than unrest and conflict.

I don't know. Maybe the onset of autumn makes me moody, more sensitive. The cream infusions for the ganache taste stronger these days. Too much coffee that I must amend with a bit more cream, which is sweet this time of year. The lavender seems cloying, so I add a bit more earthy vanilla bean, and a chocolate from Peru that is slightly more vegetal than floral. It all comes out right in the end. But it's the getting there that seems the struggle these days. More time in the means, compensating for the imbalance in my immediate surroundings.

Is summer too sweet? Fleeting, yes. And perhaps that's how Mother Nature makes up for the fast-fading paradise that Maine is in July and August. A goodness that, alas, is too good. And so we must complicate it. Bring it around to what we're used to. What it's always been. Bitter then sweet. Foiled with unrest.

And this is when recipes fail us, I suppose. The kind that we use in the kitchen, and the kind with which we govern our lives. I often boast that my ganache recipes are fool-proof. Infuse the cream, chop the chocolate, strain, boil, emulsify, spread into the frame—in which, I have calculated, it will fit perfectly. But the only constant in the recipe is that, unfailingly, each batch is different from the last. This, I have come to realize, isn't my failing as a cook, but rather the nature of the ingredients I choose to use. Natural things that are subject to changes in weather, stages of development at harvest time, the whim of the farmer, the roaster.

Sometimes people choose their communities as I would choose those ingredients, believing that the finest human beings (*our* kind of people) make fine communities. That like minds and lifestyles, accompanied by a prescribed set of rules (in the communal household I lived in years ago, they called them "habits")—a recipe, really—will guarantee utopia. But more often, and even in the planned situations, I think, communities are sprouted from the place they settle. A love of place. A fierce connection and commitment to place. And because we are people, and subject to our own storms and halcyon days; our own belligerent demons and quiet angels; this commitment manifests in vastly different ways, and so conflict and unrest are inevitable.

Not that I like it. And I find myself impatient with neighbors that I feel are being inflammatory or slanderous; unfair or bull-headed. But I am not fluent in the ways of people. And so I try to take my lesson from the lavender or the coffee. Improvise with the ingredients available. When it is too bitter, add sweetness; too floral, add earth.

Black Dinah Chocolate Tiramisu

If I'm ever asked if I have a signature dessert, this cake is my answer. It consists of four feather-light layers of chocolate genoise, generously soaked with sweet rum syrup. The cake is then filled and covered with an espresso-spiked mascarpone cream, scattered with whole coffee beans, and dusted with cocoa. The cake made its debut, wrapped in a satiny sheet of chocolate and crowned with Nancy Calvert's fragrant late-summer roses, at an all-chocolate dinner I gave at the Keeper's House several years ago. A glorious conclusion to the meal, and an irrefutable showstopper. I have since scaled down the presentation, but the cake is no less delicious because of it. SERVES 8 TO 10

....

For the soaking syrup:

½ CUP GRANULATED SUGAR

½ CUP DARK RUM

....

For the cake:

⅔ CUP FLOUR (SIFT BEFORE MEASURING)

⅔ CUP DUTCH-PROCESS COCOA (SIFT BEFORE MEASURING)

8 TABLESPOONS UNSALTED BUTTER

1 TABLESPOON VANILLA

8 LARGE EGGS

1 ⅓ CUPS GRANULATED SUGAR

....

For the frosting:

16 OUNCES MASCARPONE CHEESE

2 CUPS HEAVY CREAM

¼ CUP GRANULATED SUGAR

1 TEASPOON VANILLA

1 TABLESPOON INSTANT ESPRESSO POWDER

....

To make the syrup, combine ½ cup of water and the sugar in a saucepan. Bring the mixture to a boil over medium heat and cook until all the sugar has dissolved. Remove from heat.

Allow the syrup to cool completely, and then add the rum and stir. Store the syrup in a glass jar or plastic squeeze bottle in the refrigerator.

To make the cake, grease by hand, or spray with vegetable oil, two 9"x3" round cake pans. Line the cake pans with parchment paper.

Preheat the oven to 350 degrees.

Sift the flour and cocoa together. Re-sift three more times and set aside.

Melt the butter in a small saucepan, until it starts to bubble and a layer of foam forms on the surface. Scrape off the foam with a wide spoon and discard. Pour the melted butter into a medium-size bowl, being careful not to take the cloudy, white milk solids that remain at the bottom of the saucepan. Stir the vanilla into the clarified butter.

Meanwhile, have a pot of simmering water ready. Break the eggs into the bowl of your stand mixer, whisk in the sugar, and place the bowl over the simmering water. While stirring gently, heat the mixture until it is a little warmer than room temperature. Remove from heat and immediately begin to beat at high speed with the whisk attachment for 8 to 10 minutes. The mixture is ready when it falls in ribbons that hold their shape slightly when the whisk is lifted from the bowl. Place the bowl that contains the clarified butter over the simmering pot of water, and leave it for a minute or two while you complete the next step.

Remove the mixing bowl from its stand, and sift the flour mixture onto the surface of the egg mixture in three additions, folding with a large rubber spatula between additions. Remove the bowl of butter from the simmering pot, and pour roughly 2 cups of the batter into the butter. With a smaller spatula, fold the butter and batter together, and then return this mixture to the larger bowl of batter. Fold together.

Empty the batter into the cake pans, smoothing the top with an offset spatula. Bake for 20 to 30 minutes, or until the cake has completely come away from the sides of the pans.

Cool completely before removing the cake from the pans. To make the frosting, beat the cheese, cream, sugar, vanilla, and espresso powder in a stand mixer with the whisk attachment until the cream is smooth and spreadable. Try not to overbeat, as the mixture tends to get grainy and will eventually separate.

To assemble the cake, cut each layer in half so that you end up with four circular layers. Place one layer on your cake plate, and douse with the rum syrup (a plastic squeeze bottle works great for this). Allow the cake to soak up the syrup. Slather on a ½-inch layer of frosting, and top with the next layer. Douse this top layer with rum syrup, and then frost. Repeat this process for each layer. You will probably not use all the syrup. It will keep in the refrigerator until your next project.

Cover the entire cake with frosting (if necessary, smooth out the sides of the cake by trimming with a long bread knife before frosting). Reserve a little frosting for eight "turbans" on top of the cake. Pipe these on with a pastry bag and a large star tip.

Toss a couple whole coffee beans onto the tip of each turban, and then, using a fine sieve, dust the entire cake lightly with cocoa powder. Refrigerate and serve the cake well-chilled, accompanied by something bubbly to drink.

COOKIES
and
SWEET
SNACKS

Macarons with Chocolate Buttercream

Macarons—crisp, almond-studded, meringue sandwich cookies—made their first appearance on the island while I was recipe testing for the new cafe season several winters ago. I had been swept up in the *macaron* fad—charmed by a friend's pictures of the multi-color stacked displays of the petite cookies in bakery windows in France.

However, while experimenting, I discovered I preferred a more free-form looking meringue; and that there wasn't nearly enough filling in a traditional *macaron*.

My version gives you a lopsided, undyed—but no less charming—cookie in which the delicate meringue is the perfect delivery vehicle for a generous amount of piped chocolate buttercream. MAKES 16 TO 20

....

¾ CUP BLANCHED ALMONDS

1 ½ CUPS CONFECTIONERS' SUGAR

3 LARGE EGG WHITES, AT ROOM TEMPERATURE

¼ TEASPOON SALT

⅓ CUP GRANULATED SUGAR

¼ TEASPOON VANILLA EXTRACT

2 CUPS CHOCOLATE BUTTERCREAM (PAGES 78–79)

¼ TEASPOON ALMOND EXTRACT

....

Preheat the oven to 350 degrees. Spread the almonds on a cookie sheet and toast in the oven for 10 to 12 minutes, or until the almonds are just starting to brown and become fragrant. Remove from the oven and cool completely.

Turn the oven down to 300 degrees, and line two cookie sheets with parchment paper.

Whir the cooled almonds and the confectioners sugar in a food processor until they form a fine, crumbly mixture.

With an electric beater or a stand mixer, beat the egg whites and the salt together until they form soft peaks. Add the granulated sugar, a bit at a time, continuing to beat until the mixture holds stiff peaks.

Fold the ground almond mixture into the whites in two batches. Gently stir in the vanilla extract.

Place the meringue into a large pastry bag, and pipe 16 to 20 blobs onto each sheet pan (so that you have a total of 32 to 40 blobs). If you don't like the peaks formed by the piping, you can tamp them down with a wet finger.

Bake the meringues for 15 to 20 minutes, rotating the pans once. The meringue should look puffed and dry, and they should just have begun to burst a bit where they touch the parchment paper.

Allow the meringues to cool completely on their pans, on a cooling rack. When they are cool, gently peel them from the parchment paper and set aside.

Mix the buttercream with the almond extract, and transfer to a pastry bag fitted with a large star tip.

Pipe roughly 2 tablespoons of buttercream onto the flat side of half of the meringues. Sandwich with the other half, pressing down very gently so as not to break the delicate meringue. The meringues are best if they are served immediately. However, you may keep them at a cool room temperature, sealed in an airtight container, for several hours. Otherwise, keep them refrigerated in an airtight container, but remember to bring them back up to room temperature before serving.

Mexican Whoopie Pies

About four years ago, on a gray, early spring day, Steve and I were contemplating the slightly dismal view from our second-story office. Not just the view of our lackluster winter-worn dooryard, but also the more abstract view of a tiny, isolated community coming out of a really tough winter. The island population had taken a huge hit earlier in the fall, and by March, those of us who were left seemed to be doing all we could to keep from shooting at each other from the trees.

So, when a nice woman named Michele—half of the partnership that makes up the fabulous El El Frijoles Mexican restaurant in Sargentville—called us up later that day and asked if she and her husband, Michael, and their two friends could impose upon us for a visit later in the week, Steve and I practically begged her to come sooner.

They arrived, as promised, on a spectacular sunny day, and stranded themselves at our mercy until the next boat left seven hours later. They brought burritos and Michele's own salsa roja. I made blueberry-cream cheese scones and bacon. And we've been friends ever since.

El El Frijoles is located on the edge of a forest in Sargentville, Maine, right off Route 15, and about a ¼ mile from the Eggemoggin Country Store. This place is the very best kind of California-style cantina—squashed into a classic Maine farmhouse barn, it manifests an ironic kind of harmony perfectly suited to its quixotic creators.

A couple of years ago, Michael and Michele invited Steve and me to create a dessert for their Cinco de Mayo fiesta at the restaurant. I wanted the dessert to match the restaurant's tongue-in-cheek combining of Mexican cuisine with the very finest of Maine culture. Our Mexican Whoopie Pie is the result. MAKES 18 PIES

. . . .

For the cakes:

6½ TABLESPOONS BUTTER, AT ROOM TEMPERATURE

1 CUP DARK BROWN SUGAR

1 LARGE EGG, AT ROOM TEMPERATURE

1 TEASPOON VANILLA EXTRACT

1 TEASPOON BAKING POWDER

1 TEASPOON BAKING SODA

1 TEASPOON SALT

1 TEASPOON CINNAMON

1 TEASPOON CARDAMOM

1 TEASPOON GROUND ANCHO CHILE

¼ CUP DUTCH-PROCESS COCOA POWDER

2 CUPS FLOUR

1 CUP MILK

1 CUP

For the filling:
½ CUP CARAMEL SAUCE (PAGE 38), CHILLED
½ CUP HEAVY CREAM
8 OUNCES CREAM CHEESE, AT ROOM TEMPERATURE

Preheat the oven to 350 degrees. Line two cookie sheets with parchment paper.

In a stand mixer, cream together the butter and brown sugar. Add the egg and vanilla and beat until light.

In a separate bowl, whisk together the baking powder, baking soda, salt, cinnamon, cardamom, ancho chile, cocoa powder, and flour. Add these dry ingredients to the egg mixture alternately with the milk; a total of three additions, beginning and ending with the flour mixture.

Drop ⅛ cup-size scoops of batter onto the cookie sheets, leaving about 2 inches between each scoop.

Bake for 10 minutes, or until the cakes are puffed and spring back slightly when poked with your finger.

Remove the cakes from the oven and cool on the pans for a few minutes. Then move the cakes to a cooling rack. Cool completely before filling.

To make the filling, beat the caramel sauce, heavy cream, and cream cheese in the bowl of a stand mixer with the whisk attachment until the mixture is completely smooth and spreadable.

When the cakes are cool, generously frost half of them on the flat side, then gently sandwich with another cake. Serve with coffee or a tall glass of milk. Or, if you're feeling particularly depraved, mix up every Mainer's favorite cocktail—Allen's Coffee Brandy and milk over ice. *Ole*!

Cafe Chocolate Chip Cookies

Okay, okay. It's chocolate chip cookies. You need another recipe for chocolate chip cookies like you need a hole in the head.

But listen. I only include this because people *ask* for it. I know. I can't believe it either, but they do. I think it's that thing where you eat something in a place that is so different, and ever so slightly magical, that it just tastes better.

These cookies are like that. They're gigantic—bigger than any of us would ever dare to make at home, and they're best eaten on the trail. Or by the pond. Or on a sailboat. Or secretly, under a tree, shared with a new best friend with whom you've just completed a most excellent adventure. MAKES 20 TO 24 VERY LARGE COOKIES

....

1 ½ CUPS (3 STICKS) BUTTER

2 CUPS DARK BROWN SUGAR

½ CUP PLUS 2 TABLESPOONS MOLASSES

4 TEASPOONS VANILLA EXTRACT

½ TEASPOON BAKING POWDER

1 ½ TEASPOONS SALT

1 ½ TEASPOONS BAKING SODA

2 LARGE EGGS

4 ½ CUPS FLOUR

3 CUPS BITTERSWEET CHOCOLATE CHIPS

....

Preheat the oven to 375 degrees.

With the paddle attachment in a stand mixer, or by hand, cream together the butter, sugar, and molasses.

To this mixture, add the vanilla, baking powder, salt, and baking soda, and mix well.

Add the eggs, one at a time, mixing well after each addition.

Add the flour all at once and mix until just blended. Stir in all those chips.

Drop the dough by ¼ cupfuls onto a parchment-lined, or gently buttered, sheet pan. Bake for 18 to 20 minutes, until the cookies are lightly browned and just cooked in the center.

Chocolate-Dipped Molasses Cookies

Our most frequent visitors at the cafe are, hands down, Jeff and Judi Burke—my former employers at the Keeper's House. Jeff never misses his cup of coffee and a cinnamon bun in the morning; and not an afternoon goes by that Judi doesn't come in to check her email over a cup of tea and a cookie. And without fail, Jeff is always the first person through the door every week on Donut Day.

So, you can imagine my dismay when the pair, who now winter in the mountains of Arizona, announced upon their return to the island one spring that they had become vegan.

To say that the addition of vegan items to our cafe menu was inspired solely by what the lack of Jeff and Judi's patronage might have done to our bottom line isn't completely true. But pretty close. However, I also remember what it was like for my vegetarian husband to move to this meat-potatoes-and-seafood island all those years ago. At every potluck, someone would make a special effort to make something without meat or fish in it. It made us feel welcome, and that's exactly how we want our cafe customers to feel—whether they are longtime friends or complete strangers.

So, yes, though I don't say so in the name of this recipe, these cookies are vegan—but are adored by everyone who tries them. **MAKES 24 COOKIES**

. . . .

½ CUP COCONUT OIL

¾ CUP GRANULATED SUGAR

¼ CUP MOLASSES

¼ CUP COOLED, MASHED SWEET POTATO

1 TABLESPOON VEGETABLE OIL

2 TEASPOONS BAKING POWDER

2 CUPS FLOUR

½ TEASPOON SALT

1 ⅛ TEASPOONS BAKING SODA

1 ⅛ TEASPOONS GROUND GINGER

¾ TEASPOON CLOVES

¾ TEASPOON CINNAMON

8 OUNCES BITTERSWEET CHOCOLATE, MELTED AND TEMPERED (PAGES 28–30)

. . . .

Preheat oven to 350 degrees. Line two cookie sheets with parchment paper.

In a stand mixer, cream together the coconut oil, sugar, molasses, and sweet potato.

In a separate, small bowl, whisk together 2 tablespoons of water, vegetable oil, and baking powder. Add this to the sugar mixture.

In a medium-size bowl, sift together the flour, salt, baking soda, ginger, cloves, and cinnamon. Beat the dry ingredients into the sugar mixture, mixing until thoroughly combined.

Roll the dough into tablespoon-size balls, and place, about 2 inches apart, on the cookie sheets. Bake for 8 to 12 minutes, rotating the sheets once during baking. Remove from the oven and cool completely on racks.

When the cookies are completely cool, dip each one in the tempered chocolate, so that half the cookie is coated, and the other half is bare. Place the cookies back on the sheet pan and allow the chocolate to set before serving.

Serve with hot tea or whiskey.

CHOCOLATE-
DIPPED
MOLASSES
COOKIES,
PAGES 92–93

Flourless Peanut Butter Chocolate Chip Blondies

One day, in an effort to come up with a recipe for an energy bar that I could actually choke down, I accidentally came up with this. Not exactly what I was going for, but each day found me more in love with them than the last.

Despite the absence of flour, the bars have a super-tender, cakey texture that seems to be just barely holding on to each melty bit of chocolate.

And as far as energy? Well, for now, they get me where I want to go. MAKES 16

....

1 CUP NATURAL PEANUT BUTTER

¼ CUP RAW HONEY

1 LARGE EGG, AT ROOM TEMPERATURE

½ CUP SWEET POTATO PUREE, OR 1 BANANA, MASHED

1 TEASPOON BAKING SODA

½ TEASPOON SEA SALT

1 CUP BITTERSWEET CHOCOLATE CHIPS

....

Preheat the oven to 350 degrees. Grease and line an 8"x8" square baking pan with parchment paper.

Place the peanut butter, honey, egg, sweet potato puree, baking soda, and salt in a food processor and whir together until smooth.

Remove the blade, stir in the chips, and then scrape the mixture into the prepared pan.

Bake for 20 minutes, or until a toothpick inserted in the center of the pan comes out almost clean. Allow the blondies to cool completely before cutting into 16 portions.

ICE CREAM,
SORBETS,
and
PUDDINGS

Maine Mint Chip Ice Cream

The secret to a successful chocolate chip ice cream—whether it has mint in it or not—is the ease and pleasure we have in eating it. After finishing off a bowl of ice cream that was loaded with chocolate chips, I am slightly disappointed when I find I didn't taste a single one of them. Too often, to actually taste the chocolate in chocolate chip ice cream, you must hold a spoonful of it in your mouth and wait for the whole thing to melt away. And even then, the ice-cold chocolate is hard to savor.

I came across the solution to this in Alice Medrich's book *Bittersweet*. If you melt the chocolate, let it solidify, and then chop it and add it to your ice cream, the chocolate becomes much more cooperative in giving off its flavor. Modern ice cream makers have made this process even simpler. If you have a maker that revolves automatically and has a chute through which to pour add-ins, you can simply melt your chocolate and pour it directly into the cold custard as it freezes. The custard will immediately harden the chocolate, and the motion of the ice cream maker will break it up into "chips."

Mint tends to take over in island gardens, so frustrated gardeners trying to create some breathing room for their other crops often give me bushels of it in the late summer. I immediately dry the fresh mint on cookie sheets in the oven (no need to turn the oven on if you have a standing pilot). Then I de-stem it and store it in airtight containers.

MAKES 1 QUART

....

1 ½ CUPS WHOLE MILK

1 CUP DRIED MINT LEAVES, CRUSHED

¾ CUP GRANULATED SUGAR

2 LARGE EGGS

2 CUPS HEAVY CREAM

6 OUNCES BITTERSWEET CHOCOLATE, CHOPPED

....

Place the milk in a saucepan and bring it to a boil. Remove from the heat, add the mint, cover the pot, and allow the cream to steep for an hour or more.

Strain the milk through a fine sieve, pressing on the leaves to extract all the liquid. Return the milk to the pan, add half the sugar, and bring to a boil.

Meanwhile, whisk the eggs and the remaining sugar in a heatproof bowl.

Pour the boiling milk in a thin, steady stream onto the eggs while whisking constantly. Return the mixture to the saucepan, and heat over a low flame until the mixture thickens slightly and reaches 170 degrees. Remove from heat, and strain the mixture through a sieve into a clean bowl. Stir in the heavy cream. Refrigerate until well chilled.

Melt the chocolate in a small, heat-proof bowl, over a pan of hot water. Allow the chocolate to cool.

Freeze the custard in your ice cream maker according to the manufacturer's directions. Add the melted chocolate as the ice cream churns just before the mixture is completely frozen.

If you have an ice cream maker that is churned by hand you will need to cool the chocolate on a piece of parchment paper until it hardens (use of the refrigerator hastens this process), then chop the chocolate and add it to the custard just before it is finished freezing.

Scrape the ice cream into an airtight container, place a sheet of plastic wrap directly on the surface of it, and freeze until firm.

Mexican Chocolate Sorbet

When I was still cooking at the Keeper's House, I would make a honey-sweetened, light chocolate drink by heating milk with chile pods, cinnamon sticks, whole cloves, and vanilla beans. I would let the whole spices steep in the milk (as I do now when I flavor the cream for my ganache), strain them out, shave in a small amount of bittersweet chocolate, and add a spoonful of honey. When we were developing our sipping chocolate mix for the cafe, I finally admitted that it was impractical to package whole spices with ground chocolate and call it a "mix." So we adapted that first original recipe by replacing the whole spices with ground, and by doubling the amount of chocolate. In the summer, we chill our brewed Sipping Chocolate, and serve it over ice in tall glass mugs, topped with a frothing dollop of lightly whipped cream. One day, on a whim, I decided to instead put a quart of chilled mixture through the ice cream maker. The following is a dairy-free adaptation of that experiment. MAKES 1 ½ QUARTS

⅛ CUP HONEY

¼ CUP DUTCH-PROCESS COCOA POWDER

½ TEASPOON ANCHO CHILI POWDER

½ TEASPOON CINNAMON

A PINCH GROUND CARDAMOM

6 OUNCES BITTERSWEET CHOCOLATE, CHOPPED

1 TABLESPOON VANILLA EXTRACT

Combine 3 cups water and the honey in a medium saucepan and bring to a boil. Add the cocoa, ancho chile powder, cinnamon, and cardamom and boil for 5 minutes while whisking intermittently. Remove the saucepan from the heat.

Immediately add the chocolate to the saucepan and allow to sit for a minute or two. Then whisk the mixture until it is smooth. Transfer to a clean bowl and allow it to cool completely. When the mixture is cool, stir in the vanilla and chill for several hours.

When the mixture is chilled, freeze in an ice cream maker according to the manufacturer's instructions.

Strawberry Balsamic Sorbet
with Chocolate Black Pepper Sauce

I cannot tell you how many times I've been asked over the last ten years, "So, what do you do here in the winter?" Well, aside from producing roughly 100,000 truffles between the months of November and April, developing new marketing plans, writing books, expanding our business, and all the other countless tasks business owners all over the world have to contend with, we amuse ourselves by asking each other questions like, "If you were a superhero, what would your superpower be?" Or, "What would you do if you won the lottery?" Or my personal irony-wrought favorite: "If you were stranded on a deserted island and could only have one food to live on, what would it be?" My answers to the first two questions change from winter to winter; but my answer to the last is always the same: this sorbet. MAKES 1 ¼ QUARTS

....

1 QUART STRAWBERRY PUREE (PAGE 36)

¾ CUP GRANULATED SUGAR

1 ½ TABLESPOONS BALSAMIC VINEGAR, OR TO TASTE

8 OUNCES BITTERSWEET CHOCOLATE, CHOPPED

8 TABLESPOONS UNSALTED BUTTER

1 TABLESPOON CORN SYRUP

½ TEASPOON FRESHLY GROUND BLACK PEPPER, OR TO TASTE

PINCH OF SALT

....

Place the strawberry puree and the sugar in a medium-size saucepan and cook over medium heat just until the sugar is completely dissolved. Remove the pan from the heat and pour the mixture into a heat-proof bowl. Stir in the balsamic vinegar (I tend to taste as I go, my goal being to accent the taste of the strawberries rather than taste the vinegar).

Cover and chill the puree thoroughly.

While the puree is chilling, make the chocolate sauce. Place the chocolate, butter, corn syrup, pepper, salt, and ½ cup of water into a heat-proof bowl and set the bowl over a saucepan of just boiled water. Allow the bowl to sit until all the ingredients are melted. Stir to combine.

When the strawberry puree is completely chilled, freeze in an ice cream maker according to the manufacturer's instructions.

Serve sorbet in chilled bowls, with a generous drizzle of the warm chocolate sauce.

Broken Heart Earl Grey Truffle Ice Cream

In spite of the fact that Valentine's Day is certainly not our busiest holiday, it is still pretty slammin'; and so after a few deep breaths following Christmas, I get right on a production cycle for Valentine's Day shipping.

One year, anticipating a large number of custom orders for heart-shaped chocolates, I doubled up on the production of our Earl Grey Truffle—a tea-infused, heart-shaped confection. I made hundreds upon hundreds of them, and Steve and I packed them in their storage containers and awaited the orders. When the first orders started to come in, we opened the containers and discovered that every last one of them had cracked.

So, I made hundreds upon hundreds more. Again, a few days later, the chocolate shells on the truffles formed a large crack, leaving the chocolates, though still delicious, utterly unsellable.

Beside myself, and under the gun to produce schmaltzy romantic chocolates, I tried one more time. Again, the entire batch formed cracks after a few days in storage. So, we took the truffle off of our website, and went into Valentine's Day sans heart-shaped chocolates.

After the dust had settled from the holiday rush, I went back to my kitchen and approached the Earl Grey mystery with a fresh, unstressed mind. It turned out it was the tea I had used to infuse the cream (see the recipe for Earl Grey Truffles page 45). I had recently switched from Twining's to a delicious organic blend that I loved to drink. Unfortunately, the tea contained too much bergamot (which made it a great sipper), and the citrus oil was curdling the ganache, and as the ganache expanded inside the chocolate shell, it cracked the chocolate open.

I immediately went back to my old standby, Twining's, which solved the problem, but I still had literally hundreds and hundreds and hundreds of Earl Grey truffles that I couldn't sell.

The following recipe is the result of the ingenious suggestion from Steve to use the truffles in ice cream that summer in the café. And so we did.

You don't have to put the truffles in the ice cream; it's just as good unadulterated, with a good dose of chocolate sauce drizzled on top. **Makes about 1 quart**

. . . .

1 ½ CUPS WHOLE MILK

¼ CUP EARL GREY TEA LEAVES

4 LARGE EGG YOLKS

¾ CUP GRANULATED SUGAR

2 CUPS HEAVY CREAM

1 CUP EARL GREY TRUFFLES, CHOPPED

. . . .

Place the milk in a medium-size saucepan and bring to a boil. Once it boils, remove from the heat, add the tea leaves, and cover. Allow the milk to steep for 5 minutes.

Meanwhile, whisk the yolks and half the sugar in a heat-proof bowl.

Strain the milk and put it back in the saucepan with the remaining sugar, and bring it to a boil.

Pour the boiling milk in a thin steady stream onto the yolks while whisking constantly. Return the mixture to the saucepan, and heat over a low flame until the mixture thickens slightly and reaches 170 degrees. Remove from the heat, pour the mixture into a clean bowl, and add the heavy cream. Refrigerate until well chilled.

Freeze the custard in your ice cream maker according to the manufacturer's directions. Add the chopped truffles just before the mixture is completely frozen.

Scrape the ice cream into an air-tight container, place a sheet of plastic wrap directly on the surface of it, and freeze until firm.

Bittersweet Chocolate Pudding

Though my single mother did an admirable job of keeping us kids fueled-up on unprocessed foods and fresh vegetables, she had a few breaking points. They were: canned tomato soup, boxed macaroni and cheese, and Jell-O instant pudding. In fact, I remember more than a few post-work Monday-night meals that consisted of exactly these three items. Occasionally, even now as an adult, if I'm feeling like I need a little comfort food, these are my instant stand-bys. Luckily, the island store happens to stock all of these items, but even I can admit that there is nothing like pudding made from scratch. All the comfort, none of the chemicals. SERVES 6 TO 8

....

⅔ CUP GRANULATED SUGAR

¼ CUP CORN STARCH

½ TEASPOON SALT

4 LARGE EGG YOLKS

3 CUPS MILK

5 OUNCES BITTERSWEET CHOCOLATE, CHOPPED AND MELTED

2 OUNCES UNSWEETENED CHOCOLATE, CHOPPED AND MELTED

2 TABLESPOONS UNSALTED BUTTER

1 TEASPOON VANILLA EXTRACT

....

In a medium-size saucepan, whisk together the sugar, corn starch, salt, and egg yolks until smooth. Whisk in the milk, and then place the pan over medium heat and cook, stirring constantly, until the mixture boils.

Simmer for 1 minute, and then remove from the heat. Press this hot mixture through a sieve into a heat-proof bowl, and then stir in the chocolates, butter, and vanilla. Mix thoroughly until everything is melted and the pudding is smooth.

Press a sheet of plastic wrap directly on the surface of the pudding and place in the refrigerator to chill thoroughly.

Serve the pudding in parfait glasses with a dollop of lightly sweetened whipped cream.

Feelin' the love

"Here's the thing about Valentine's Day," I heard myself telling our sales rep at one of our suppliers one January day. She had just asked me if we were gearing up for a busy February.

"It's about the men," I continued. "Most gifts bought for Valentine's Day are bought by men. So do you know what that means?"

The sales rep was no dummy. "It means they're bought on February fourteenth," she said without a moment's hesitation.

"Exactly. So mail-order chocolates, no matter how romantic or delicious, get the shaft."

And though every fiber of my California/feminist/liberal upbringing roars against such stereotypes, facts are facts. I mean these things have been studied. And, frankly, I've found it extremely helpful to my marriage, to friendships, and just to life in general, to understand these innate characteristics that are sometimes defined by, if not exactly, biology, then at the very least, gender association. For instance, imagine my incredible relief when I discovered that MOST men leave their dirty socks all over the house, and not just my husband. He wasn't doing it specifically to annoy me! Hallelujah!

But I digress.

To be honest, until I moved to a cold climate, I had just never been all that into Valentine's Day. Don't get me wrong: I can wax poetic about love and heartbreak with the best of 'em—but a holiday that leaves just as many people feeling lonely and sad as loved and appreciated? I just can't go for that.

But then I came to Maine. And those of you who live, or have lived, in the frozen Northeast know that February is a cruel, cold, heartless month. It's windy and icy and a wee bit lonely—by this time the snow has lost its charm, and most folks are pretty sick of digging out to socialize face to face.

But then comes Valentine's Day—a day that, at least in these parts, not so much celebrates romantic love, but warmth—literal and metaphorical.

Last Tuesday, after a blizzardy game night at the cafe, Lisa, Marion Drew, Bel MacDonald, and I watched as the rest of the crew worked to get island newcomer Louise's truck out of the snowbank it was stuck in. We were sipping the dregs of our tea while chatting about the state of my kitchen, which was in the throes of Valentine's Day production.

"I have to tell you something," Marion said in her upbeat, conversational way. "My Lenny died on Valentine's Day, and it's ruined it for me ever since." And though she says this with a wistful smile, it's hard to believe that much could ruin this powerful woman's positive attitude, immense sense of humor, and her no-nonsense dealings with the world and its hardships—whether it's raising nine kids, or having frozen pipes in January, or coping with a loving husband's momentary lapse in consideration when he dies on Valentine's Day.

But love is like that. As much as it has the power to heal and heat, it also has the power to tear our hearts apart.

Meanwhile, Alison has tied Louise's truck to the rear bumper of her burly Jeep and, with the help of islanders ranging in age from eleven to sixty pushing in the blizzard, pulls it from the snowbank.

It's all a rush after that: people shuffling around the cars, trying to get out of the driveway before they get stuck again, punctuated with hurried goodbyes. And later, as I was washing up the last of the teacups, I was struck again by this tiny population bringing their collective warmth to my home—and to each other. Making an effort to be in the physical presence of each other, whether it's Tuesday night game nights, Wednesday library hours, Thursday night Knitting Society, monthly book club, or just getting together for a warm meal with neighbors. In an era of email and Facebook, Skype and countless forms of remote communication, I think it's quite an accomplishment that our little community has the energy and desire to be *together*.

Black Bread Pudding with Tangerine Compote

I like this dark, dense pudding without the addition of the optional chopped chocolate. It's dark and mysterious, and richly satisfying. But the chocolate adds a frame of reference to the otherwise unexplained dark color of the custard-softened bread.

SERVES 9

For the pudding:

8 CUPS CUBED BLACK BREAD (PAGES 125–126)

1 QUART MILK

4 LARGE EGGS

1 CUP GRANULATED SUGAR

1/8 TEASPOON CLOVES

1/2 TEASPOON CINNAMON

1/4 CUP DARK RUM, OPTIONAL

2 TEASPOONS VANILLA EXTRACT

1 CUP CHOPPED CHOCOLATE OR CHOCOLATE CHIPS, OPTIONAL

For the compote:

4 TANGERINES

1/4 CUP GRANULATED SUGAR

1 CINNAMON STICK

3 WHOLE CLOVES

Preheat oven to 350 degrees. Generously butter a 9" square baking pan.

In a large bowl, whisk together milk, eggs, sugar, cloves, cinnamon, rum, and vanilla. Add the bread and stir, submerging it in the liquid. Allow the mixture to sit for an hour or so.

While the bread is soaking, make the compote. With a very sharp knife, cut away the peel and the pith from the tangerines. While holding a tangerine over a small saucepan, carefully remove each section by cutting them out with your knife. Let the fruit and any escaping juice fall into the saucepan as you cut. Try not to take the membrane that encases each section of the fruit. Repeat with all four tangerines.

Add the sugar, cinnamon stick, cloves, and a little water to get things going (about 2 tablespoons). Cook very gently on low heat while stirring, until the sugar dissolves and the mixture just begins to bubble. Remove from the heat, cover, and allow the mixture to steep until you're ready to serve the pudding.

Return to your bread pudding. Stir in the chopped chocolate and then scrape the whole gloppy mess into the baking pan.

Bake for 30 to 40 minutes, or until a knife inserted in the middle of the pudding comes out clean.

Cool the pudding for 10 minutes or so, cut into 9 squares, and serve in wide bowls, with the compote ladled over the top. A scoop of vanilla ice cream wouldn't go amiss here, either.

Cocoa Nib Crème Brûlée

Ownership of a blowtorch on the island is as requisite as owning a chainsaw, several full gas cans, and a spare car that doesn't run any more. You just never know when a pipe is going to burst and you'll need to solder a repair. In the fall, you may be on your way to a friend's house for dinner, only to find your way blocked by a fallen tree. No need to miss dinner; the chainsaw is in the back of your truck, fueled and at the ready. As is a filled gas can, precaution against running out of fuel when the one store on the island is not open in the winter. The spare car exists solely to provide parts for repairs to your working car, in the absence of an on-island auto shop.

Other than pristine coastline, a treasured way of life, and an abundance of the freshest and tastiest seafood in the world, the island has very few luxuries to offer. But I consider crème brûlée a necessity. So when I informed Jeff and Judi, my employers at the Keeper's House, that crème brûlée would be in regular rotation on our dessert menu, they were dubious. And when I asked Jeff if I could borrow a blowtorch from his workshop, they were puzzled. But when I presented them with dessert that night, they were thrilled—and, I like to think, assured that they had hired the right woman for the job.

You will need a blowtorch to complete this recipe. If you don't have one, borrow one from a self-sufficient neighbor. **SERVES 8 TO 10**

....

1 VANILLA BEAN

1 QUART HEAVY CREAM, PLUS A LITTLE MORE FOR TOPPING OFF

2 CUPS COCOA NIBS

4 LARGE EGGS

4 LARGE EGG YOLKS

¾ CUP GRANULATED SUGAR, PLUS MORE FOR GARNISH

....

Split and scrape the vanilla bean and place the seeds and the pod in a medium-size saucepan with the cream and the cocoa nibs. Bring the cream mixture to a boil. Remove the pan from the heat, cover, and allow the mixture to steep for an hour or more.

Preheat the oven to 325 degrees, and bring a kettle of water to a boil.

Strain the cream, discarding the solids, and add additional cream to bring the total amount back up to 4 cups. Pour the cream back into the saucepan, and heat over a medium flame until it just begins to boil.

Meanwhile, whisk together the eggs, egg yolks, and sugar in a large, heat-proof bowl. When the cream reaches a boil, pour it into the egg mixture in a thin steady stream, whisking the entire time.

Pour the custard into one-cup custard dishes, place the dishes in a roasting a pan, and pour the boiling water into the pan so that it comes halfway up the sides of the custard dishes.

Bake the custards for 20 to 25 minutes, or until the edges have set but they are still wiggly in the middle. Try not to over-bake, otherwise your eggs will curdle and the custard won't be smooth.

Remove the custards from the water bath, cool, and then chill thoroughly.

When you are ready to serve the crème brûlées, take them from the refrigerator and sprinkle a thin coating of granulated sugar on top.

Light the blowtorch, and cook the sugar on top of the custards by moving the torch flame smoothly and evenly back and forth across the surface of the sugar. The sugar will melt and bubble and turn a dark golden brown. Kill the torch, allow a few seconds for the sugar to harden, and serve immediately with good strong coffee.

A FEW
SAVORIES

Roast Chicken with
New England–Style Mole Poblano

Show me a person who doesn't like the movie *Chocolat*, and I'll show you a person with no *joie de vivre*, no heart. I always felt a little sheepish admitting that I do actually really love this movie—and, in fact, would consider it among my favorites. The chocolate thing is merely the frosting on a cake that is, admittedly, mostly frosting; and which includes such lip-smacking bonuses as sexy river pirate Johnny Depp, Grande Dame Judi Dench, Juliette Binoche with her perfect accent *and* perfectly accented in a red cape, draped in the gorgeous, textured folds of magical realism and small-town politics in a storybook village. I felt slightly embarrassed, given my situation, that if I admitted my attachment to this movie, people might think I was equating myself with beautiful Vianne Rocher and her skill with people and chocolate. I worried about this until I discovered that most people actually (much to my disappointment) *don't* think of this movie when they hear I make chocolate in a small village on the coast of Maine. Instead, they say, "Oh, you make chocolate? Like Willy Wonka!"

I find this horrifying. *Charlie and the Chocolate Factory* was one of those movies that haunted me all through my adolescence. The freaky house with the edible wallpaper might as well have been a haunted mansion, and the image of that girl blowing up like a huge blue beach ball gave me nightmares for years. The remake that came out a few years ago, instead of erasing those images, just added to the pile. Johnny Depp's Willy Wonka is, arguably, one of the creepiest movie characters of all time.

Here's the thing about Juliette Binoche's character in *Chocolat*: Vianne is not just a staggeringly gorgeous chocolateur, but also an amazing cook. Who can forget the dinner party she throws for Armande? And that silky, dark mole she ladles over roasted hens. It is that singular image that inspired the following recipe.

There are, admittedly, an astonishing number of ingredients in this recipe. But if you begin by reading through the recipe carefully, and then organize your time and your space accordingly, you will be rewarded with a very special dish. **SERVES 6**

- -

8 WHOLE GARLIC CLOVES

3 MEDIUM FRESH TOMATOES

1 MEDIUM WHITE OR YELLOW ONION, SLICED

3 TABLESPOONS OLIVE OIL

8 ANCHO CHILES, OR OTHER MILD, MEDIUM-SIZE, DARK RED DRIED CHILES

¼ CUP SHELLED WALNUTS

¼ CUP DRIED CRANBERRIES

2 SLICES WHITE BREAD, CUBED

1 CUP APPLE CIDER

½ CUP PUMPKIN PUREE (PAGE 36) OR CANNED PUMPKIN

1 ½ OUNCES MEXICAN CHOCOLATE, CHOPPED

½ TEASPOON CINNAMON

⅛ TEASPOON GROUND CLOVES

¼ TEASPOON GROUND CUMIN

1 ½ TEASPOONS DRIED OREGANO

ABOUT 6 CUPS CHICKEN OR TURKEY STOCK, WARMED

GRANULATED SUGAR, TO TASTE

SALT, TO TASTE

ONE (4-POUND) ROASTING CHICKEN

FRESHLY GROUND BLACK PEPPER, TO TASTE

1 TEASPOON BUTTER, FOR THE ROASTING PAN

1 TABLESPOON SESAME SEEDS

....

Preheat the oven to 400 degrees. Peel the garlic cloves, leaving the cloves whole. Core the tomatoes and slice them into thick wedges. Toss the tomatoes, garlic, and sliced onions with 2 tablespoons of the olive oil in a large bowl. Spill the vegetables out onto a cookie sheet and roast in the oven for 30 to 40 minutes, or until the garlic and onions are golden and the tomatoes have deflated.

While the vegetables are roasting, stem and de-seed the chiles and tear them into 1-inch pieces. Scatter them onto a cookie sheet with the walnuts, cranberries, and bread, and roast in the oven for about 10 minutes, or until the chiles and nuts begin to smell fragrant. Remove them from the oven and slide all the ingredients off the cookie sheet into a heatproof bowl.

In a small saucepan, bring the apple cider to a boil over medium heat. When the cider boils, pour it immediately over the chile mixture and allow to it sit for 15 minutes. Place the soaked ingredients into the bowl of your food processor.

When the vegetables are done roasting, scoop them into the food processor with the chile mixture. Add the pumpkin puree, chocolate, cinnamon, cloves, cumin, oregano, and ½ cup warm stock to the ingredients in the food processor. Grind everything together until you have a loose paste. Add more stock if necessary.

Next, push the paste through a medium sieve, or put it through the medium attachment of a food mill.

Heat the remaining tablespoon of oil in a wide skillet over medium-high heat. Scrape the strained paste into the pan and cook until it is very thick and darkens slightly. Add the remaining stock, stir to blend, partially cover the pan, and simmer for about 45 minutes. Season the sauce with granulated sugar and salt to taste.

Preheat the oven to 350 degrees.

Rinse, dry, then quarter the chicken. Separate the thighs from the drumsticks, and rub down all of it with salt and pepper.

Butter a large roasting pan. Heat the remaining tablespoon of olive oil in a large, heavy skillet over medium-high heat. When the pan is very hot, brown the chicken pieces on all sides, and remove them to the roasting pan. Pour the mole over the chicken, cover the pan with foil, pop in the oven, and bake for about an hour and a half, or until the meat is soft and a bit of it pulls very easily from the bones.

While the chicken is baking, toast the sesame seeds in a small skillet over medium heat until they begin to pop and become fragrant. Set aside.

Serve the chicken on warmed plates, in a pool of sauce and sprinkled with the toasted sesame seeds. I recommend providing a basket of warm tortillas and a side dish of roasted sweet potatoes.

Alternatively, pull the chicken from the bones, and stir the meat into the mole. Allow guests to make their own soft tacos with the shredded chicken, roasted sweet potatoes, and some shredded green cabbage.

A Postcard from Home

There is nothing quite like the feeling of returning home after a long journey. In my case, the humbleness of my home or the greatness of the place I'd just been never seem to matter; the part of my heart that attaches itself to this familiar space blinds me to the dishes left in the sink in the rush of leaving, or to the light bulbs that unfailingly burn out when no one is there to watch them.

A powerful phenomenon, this, especially since it seems to happen regardless of what sort of messes await my return. I imagine this feeling is similar to a woman's ability to forget the pain of childbirth when she discovers she is expecting another baby. The joy of discovering anew a familiar space or experience overrides any trepidation.

I left the island two weeks ago. The car weather radio threatened an impending blizzard during my entire drive to the airport. The plane took off just as the first flakes began to fall, and I accepted a watery, tepid Styrofoam cup of coffee from the flight attendant with an enormous smile on my face.

And who wouldn't be smiling? I was headed straight to the high deserts of New Mexico, which boasts 350 days of sun per year. My Uncle Gabriel, who has been living a cushy retired life in Las Cruces since 1995, says that figure is more like 365 days.

Can you imagine feeling the sun on your face every day for fifteen years? The thought might make a proud New England curmudgeon shrink back in horror. But for me, a transplanted California girl, the idea of unlimited access to sunshine is a fantasy that can quite possibly bring me to tears given the right conditions— like the coast of Maine in, say, February.

So I spent a week basking on the outdoor patios of Mexican restaurants, hiking among the high desert canyons, and returning the overtly friendly greetings from the tanned and smiling faces of the locals.

"Why are they happy?" my uncle, a recovering New Englander himself, is fond of asking.

I gazed out his floor-to-ceiling windows as I sipped a frosty mug of beer; I looked beyond his shimmering aqua blue swimming pool, and over the pointy heads of desert cacti and mesquite, and just above the crest of the Organ

Mountains, where a huge fireball of sun was painting the desert in oranges and pinks. My uncle spreads his arms wide and shrugs his shoulders as if to say, "Isn't it obvious?"

As the blizzards continued in Maine that week, I was oblivious, sitting in a cheerfully busy Mesilla restaurant, devouring a steaming plate of chile rellenos smothered in spicy New Mexican chile verde sauce.

While Steve was home, minding the post-Valentine orders and shoveling our porches and paths leading to and from the woodpile, I was spending a lazy hour gazing at a swelling New Mexican moon from the stoop of a brightly painted pottery shop.

And as my fellow islanders woke up the morning after the worst of the storm had shoved off, assessed the damage from their living room windows, and then finally decided to keep their pajamas on, I was just hearing the news from my uncle's television.

So did I immediately start jumping up and down on the sofa, rejoicing in the fact that I was missing winter's last knife-in-the-gut blast of horrid weather? Did I have the sudden urge to call and lord it over my snowed-in neighbors on the island? Was I exchanging high-fives with my uncle and heckling the shivering newscasters reporting from the coast of Maine?

Not exactly.

Instead, a very odd sensation began to take hold of me. I suddenly felt unexpectedly, and decidedly, homesick.

A few days later, I flew out of El Paso around the time that my neighbors were beginning to dig themselves out of their houses and unbury their cars. I arrived at the mailboat dock in Stonington the next morning to find a good-natured Garrett Aldrich shoveling out my parking space.

When the quiet winter boat docked at Isle au Haut forty-five minutes later, the familiar scene of islanders picking up supplies, or getting ready to do some shopping on the mainland after a week of being cooped up, made me smile. And when I arrived home to a shoveled porch, a wood-warmed house, and a basket of Lisa Turner's oatmeal chocolate chip cookies on my dining room table, I felt happier than I'd felt in weeks.

Just before sunset, Steve and I set out on a walk through the island winter wonderland. Though porches were shoveled and the roads clear, the new snow was still high and smooth in the yards and along the edges of the island forest. A couple of the school kids were having a raucous snowball fight in front of the tiny post office, and as we walked up the town hall hill, the friendly, booming voice of Bill Clark called from a window, inviting us in for a warm-up. Later, walking west and back towards home, we were just in time to watch a tangerine winter sun escape below an undulating horizon of blue water and lobster boats.

Later that week, after tackling and reacquainting myself with my abandoned work-load, I began a thank-you note to my aunt and uncle. I included a photo of my smiling self, shoveling a path to the laundry line in the hip-deep snow. On the back of the picture I penned my uncle's favorite question: "Why is this woman happy?"

I thought of how I might describe the landscape of this small island. What it feels like to come home to the kindness of neighbors. What it's like to live among people who were born in the same house where they still live, whose children go to the same school they went to, who think nothing of giving a casual wave to their great-grandmothers as they walk to the store, or put up the morning mail. How can I explain to my uncle why it makes sense for us all to have a key to the town's library so that we may check out a book at a moment's notice? Or why all local calls from the island's two pay phones are free?

It occurred to me that places like this are as rare and fragile as all the wild places of the earth. And we are at just as much risk of losing them. Forever. I think of telling my uncle this, on this too-small thank-you card. I long to beg him and my aunt to come for a visit and meet this place I call home and this community full of people I call friends before it's too late.

I look again at the picture of myself shivering giddily amid the ice and snow. Why is she happy? Instead, I write, "Isn't it obvious?"

Filo Cigars with Cabrales Cheese, Bittersweet Chocolate, and Sherry Dipping Sauce

When I was a senior in high school, I spent a year in Istanbul, Turkey, as an exchange student. Every afternoon when my host sisters and I returned from school, my host mother and aunts spread out a tea that included tiny cured fishes, black olives, white cheeses, charred eggplants, and a variety of *börek* in every shape and size. My favorites were the little *sigara böreks* filled with tangy *beyaz penir* (a Turkish-style feta), pan-fried in oil. Years later, when challenged to come up with an appetizer to serve at an all-chocolate dinner at the Keeper's House, I decided to pair an earthy Spanish blue cheese with bittersweet chocolate, and roll the mixture up like the little cigar-shaped pastries I loved so much from that life-changing year in the City of Seven Hills.

SERVES 8 TO 10 AS AN APPETIZER

....

1 PACKAGE FROZEN FILO DOUGH, THAWED

4 OUNCES CABRALES CHEESE, OR DOMESTIC BLUE CHEESE, AT ROOM TEMPERATURE

4 OUNCES CREAM CHEESE, AT ROOM TEMPERATURE

FRESHLY GROUND BLACK PEPPER, TO TASTE

SEA SALT, TO TASTE

2 TABLESPOONS OLIVE OIL

2 OUNCES BITTERSWEET CHOCOLATE, CHOPPED

SAFFLOWER OIL FOR FRYING

½ CUP APRICOT OR PEACH JAM

¼ CUP DRY SHERRY

....

Remove the stack of filo from the package, unfurl, and cover with a slightly damp, clean dish towel.

With a fork, mash the blue cheese and the cream cheese together in a small bowl, and season with a little pepper and salt.

Remove one sheet of filo from the stack and lay it on the countertop, with the longer end closest to you. Brush the whole thing with olive oil. Lay another sheet on top of the first. Brush with olive oil.

Cut the stacked sheets vertically into thirds.

Spread about 1 tablespoon of the cheese filling along the width of each section of the filo on the end closest to you. Place a few bits of chopped chocolate on top of the cheese.

Roll the filo into a cigar, pausing in the middle of the sheet to fold the ends in, so that the filling is completely encased in filo. Place the cigar on a cookie sheet and repeat this process with the remaining two sections of filo. Continue to stack, cut, fill, and roll filo until all the cheese and chocolate is used up.

Pour about 1½ inches of safflower oil into a wide, heavy skillet and heat on medium-high heat until the oil reaches 350 on an instant-read thermometer. Fry the cigars in several batches, turning once, until they are golden and crispy. Drain them on paper towels.

In a small saucepan, heat the jam and the sherry together until warm. Season with salt and pepper and pour into a small bowl.

Place the bowl of dipping sauce in the middle of a large dinner plate. Arrange the cigars around the bowl in a sunburst. Serve immediately.

Black Bread

At 3 A.M. on July 2, 2009, the phone rang. It probably rang twenty times before I came-to enough to find it in my dark bedroom and answer it. The voice on the other end was short and to the point: "The Cogan house is burning."

"What?" I replied, and then stupidly, "Are you kidding?"

"The Cogan house is burning," repeated Sue MacDonald, with all the patience of a person who has spent the last hour waking up sleepy people to report an emergency. "Everyone's at the fire station," she reported succinctly, and then unceremoniously hung up.

It had been a terrifying night of torrential rain and violent thunderstorms, keeping me awake and huddled in my bedroom until well past midnight. I rubbed the sleep from my eyes, got dressed, and walked out into the storm.

As luck would have it, the Cogan house was located right across the street from the fire station, and as I crested the hill above the town dock, I could see the terrifying glow of a raging fire. I parked my truck at the town hall and inserted myself into the chaos.

It took the rest of the night and into the late morning for the fire to burn the house beyond repair, despite the island's best efforts. When the smoke cleared, the crew of carpenters who had been renovating the handsome home for close to a year sat stunned and silent, having watched all their hard work go up in flames.

And then, a week later, they began to rebuild it.

On August 1, 2010, the Cogan family threw an enormous housewarming party for the community who had watched their dream home go through, not one, but two remarkable transformations. Heavily assisted by a crew of island cooks and helpful neighbors, I prepared a staggering menu for the party. Alongside island lobster salad, crab cakes, plates laden with local cheeses and fresh fruit, tiny slices of chocolate tiramisu, and dainty portions of strawberry shortcake; we served this black bread, sliced and topped with locally smoked salmon, mustard-dill sauce, and farmstand cucumbers.

MAKES 1 LARGE ROUND LOAF

2½ TEASPOONS INSTANT YEAST

1½ CUPS WHITE FLOUR

1 CUP RYE FLOUR

½ CUP PUMPERNICKEL FLOUR

2 TABLESPOONS DUTCH-PROCESS COCOA POWDER

¼ CUP MOLASSES

½ CUP STRONG BREWED COFFEE

2 TABLESPOONS UNSALTED BUTTER, MELTED

1 ½ TEASPOONS SALT

1 LARGE EGG WHITE

POPPY SEEDS

....

Place the yeast, flours, cocoa, molasses, 1 cup warm water, coffee, butter, and salt in a stand mixer and knead with the dough hook attachment, adding up to ½ cup more white flour as needed to make a smooth, slightly sticky dough. Knead for 8 to 10 minutes.

Place the dough in a greased bowl and cover with plastic wrap. Allow the dough to rise for about an hour.

After the dough has risen, punch it down and then shape it into a large ball and place the ball on lightly greased sheet pan. Dust the top with flour, cover with plastic wrap, and let it rest for 45 minutes.

Preheat the oven to 350 degrees. Beat the egg white with a tablespoon of water in a small bowl until foamy, and then brush this "wash" all over the surface of the dough. Sprinkle the loaf with poppy seeds. Cut an X into the top of the loaf, and bake for about 40 minutes.

The best way to tell if the bread is done is by removing the sheet pan from the oven, picking the loaf up with a mitted hand, and rapping the underside with your knuckle. The loaf should make a hollow "thump."

Acknowledgments

I must begin by thanking my editor Kathleen Fleury. Her out-of-the-box thinking, tenaciousness, and tender balance of flattery and tough talk made this book a reality—and its author a slightly better person.

Stacey Cramp is a truly gifted photographer who sees the beauty in the everyday mess of a working kitchen. And then turns it into art.

Warm thanks to Linda Greenlaw, whose friendship and advice helped me to believe that publishing a book is totally worth the hard work of writing it.

My heartfelt gratitude to Lisa Turner, who continues to "learn" me that it's not just about feeding people; but feeding them what they love.

Thank you, Terri Patchen, for spending 8 hours copy editing on the very first day of your vacation on the island.

And a thousand times a thousand thanks to Dianna Dewitt, Alison Richardson, Abigail Hiltz, Sarai Johnson, Bill and Brenda Clark, Diana Santospago, Jeff and Judi Burke, Kathie Fiveash, Albert Gordon, and Nancy and Bill Calvert for their love and friendship and support—and good wine—all of which are necessary for a winter of writing and editing.

No one person has contributed more to this book than the collective community of Isle au Haut—those friends and neighbors who have taught me that a place is only made perfect by all of its imperfections.

Recipe Index